STANDARD LOAN

UNLESS RECALLED BY ANOTHER READER
THIS ITEM MAY BE BORROWED FOR

FOUR WEEKS

To renew, telephone:
01243 816089 (Bishop Otter)
01243 816099 (Bognor Regis)

11. MAR 98

By the same author

Marxism and the Theory of Praxis (Lawrence and Wishart, 1975)
Marxism, Revolution and Democracy (B.R. Gruner, 1983)
The Gramscian Challenge (Basil Blackwell, 1984)

State, Power and Democracy

Contentious Concepts in Practical Political Theory

John Hoffman

Senior Lecturer in Politics
University of Leicester

WHEATSHEAF BOOKS · SUSSEX

ST. MARTIN'S PRESS · NEW YORK

First published in Great Britain in 1988 by
WHEATSHEAF BOOKS LTD
16 Ship Street, Brighton, Sussex
A Division of
Simon & Schuster International Group

and in the USA by
ST. MARTIN'S PRESS, INC.
175 Fifth Avenue, New York, NY 10010

Printed and bound in Great Britain by
Billing & Sons Limited, Worcester

British Library Cataloguing in Publication Data
Hoffman, John, *1944—*
State, power and democracy: contentious
concepts in practical political theory.
1. Political science
I. Title
320
ISBN 0-7450-0297-8
ISBN 0 7450 0299 4 Pbk

Library of Congress Cataloging-in-Publication Data
Hoffman, John, 1944—
State, power, and democracy: contentious concepts
in practical political theory/John Hoffman.
        p.   cm.
"Wheatsheaf books."
Bibliography: p.
Includes index.
ISBN 0-312-01950-5 : $30.00 (est.)
1. State, The.   2. Power (Social sciences)
3. Democracy. I. Title
JC325.H625   1988
320.5—dc19   87—35304
                                    CIP

1   2   3   4   5   92   91   90   89   88

To my Father and the Memory of my Mother

It is characteristic of the whole *grobianism* [i.e. boorishness] of 'sound common sense', which feeds upon the 'fulness of life' and does not stunt its *natural* faculties with any philosophical or other studies, that where it succeeds in seeing *differences*, it does not see *unity*, and where it sees *unity*, it does not see *differences*. If it propounds *differentiated determinants*, they at once become fossilised in its hands, and it can see only the most reprehensible sophistry, when these wooden concepts are knocked together so that they catch fire.

(Marx, 1847)

Contents

Preface

I have written this book as a (I hope not entirely eccentric) text for students of political theory. Much of the material here has been tried and tested in lectures, and I have greatly benefitted from the—let me stress, studiously solicited—interjections and interruptions of final-year undergraduates. Anyone who lectures on subjects as contentious as those discussed in this work should take to heart Marx's dictum that 'the educator needs to be educated', for although some of the arguments advanced here may appear startling and outlandish (few of my students ever agree with them!), they are a product of listening as well as lecturing.

I am grateful to the University of Leicester and the Department of Politics for providing me with a sabbatical term for writing, and I am particularly indebted to John Day and Nick Rennger for reading some of the draft chapters. Thanks are also due to the University's Research Board for a grant to defray some of the costs of a trip in 1986 to my native Zimbabwe, which helped (I think) to clarify ideas about democracy.

Much time has been spent in the common room trying to persuade one of my departmental colleagues, Murray Forsyth, of the need to get rid of the state. Like so many professional students of the subject, he remains unmoved by the case for a 'transcendental' politics. Why study institutions and practices that deserve to disappear?

This is at least one of the questions which this book tries to answer.

Leicester, September 1987

Introduction

A CONTENTIOUS TRIAD OF CONTESTABLE CONCEPTS

'The spirit of the age encourages us to be absolutist'—the anxious words of a Tory politician (Pym, 1984). Over the last ten years, politicians of the centre have begun to deplore the rise of 'conviction' or 'ideological' politics. The broad consensus about fundamental principles, which has been such a striking feature of post-war politics in much of Western Europe, now appears frayed and frazzled. Public debate increasingly turns not merely on questions of detailed policy, but upon rival *concepts*. Moreover, a novel aspect of the present situation lies in the fact that a new level of conceptual debate has been initiated by the Right rather than by the Left. Slogans like 'rolling back the frontiers of the state', 'making the trade unions democratic', or 'giving power back to the people through privatisation' have had the effect of focussing debate around conflicts of principle. As a consequence, many see in 'Thatcherism' or 'Reaganism' an attempt by the New Right to alter the way in which we actually *think* about politics, and to entrench an old-fashioned liberalism as the new orthodoxy.

This book sets out to explore three of the concepts which are central to current argument and debate: the state, power and democracy. As public controversy has become more obviously conceptual in character, the centrality of these ideas has come to the fore, both as political footballs in their own right, and as contentious concepts closely related to one another. 'Rolling back the frontiers of the *state*', 'making the unions more

1

democratic', or 'giving *power* back to the people' are slogans in which each concept is contentiously interpreted in a way which reinforces the impact of the other two. The notion that privatising public concerns, for example, gives people more 'power' also stakes out a particular view of 'state' and 'democracy'. Our three concepts are not only contentious: they also interrelate.

This interrelationship can be easily seen if we adopt a more academic view of the three concepts. Take Max Weber's celebrated definition of the state as the institution which claims a monopoly of 'legitimate force' over a given territory (1964, p. 156). Here we see right away not only a definition of the state, but also a reference to the problem of power. How can power be 'legitimate' if it also implies an element of force? This in turn raises the question: what is democracy? If the state involves hierarchy, and power involves (at least some) force, where does the concept of 'popular rule' fit in? Naturally we shall be probing these questions in detail later, but they are alluded to here merely to demonstrate that each of our three concepts has a direct bearing on the other two. We see this both in the way they appear in public debate, and when we encounter them in academic theory. This is why I refer to state, power and democracy as a contentious triad of contestable concepts.

POLITICAL THEORY AND POLITICAL PRACTICE

This point, however, raises a problem. Given the fact that these concepts are so contentious—both as ideas in their own right and as ideas which relate to one another—are they susceptible to academic analysis at all? Concepts like these have often been called 'contestable' (Gallie, 1955; Lukes, 1974, and for a more recent critique, Gray, 1983), because they seem to be inherently prone to ideological dispute, and never was this more true than it is today. The controversial nature of our three concepts raises a basic question about political theory itself: its relationship to political practice, and the practical political positions of those who argue about concepts. Are academics politically partisan when they theorise about politics? Is it possible to analyse concepts like state, power and democracy in an uncontroversial or in a non-ideological manner?

In the 1950s and 1960s it was fashionable in Britain and the United States to insist that political theory can exist as a properly academic enterprise only when it is sharply divorced from practical politics; when it is rigorously non-partisan in character. To be truly scientific or authentically philosophical, political theory must not itself be an activity which is political. Two related schools of thought argued this case.

Linguistic philosophers claimed that philosophers are competent to tackle only what are called 'second order problems' (Weldon, 1956), which means basically that while we can analyse the *words* politicians use to describe their activity, we cannot directly examine this activity itself. Analysing politics at first hand would make it impossible to sort out the linguistic muddles and confusions which politics involves, since a 'first order' examination imports into the realm of theory the conflicts and disputes of the practical world. No adequately philosophical analysis of politics is possible if theorists seek to understand (let alone transform) political reality *itself*.

Unlike linguistic philosophers, behavioural political scientists do seem willing to analyse practical politics, but the political realities which the behaviouralists examine are conceptualised as mere 'events' or 'behavioural patterns' which can be studied in a detached and disinterested manner. 'Subjective' value judgments are to be avoided by making empirically testable propositions drawn from passive (albeit rigorously researched) data, and hence, for this reason, behaviouralists believe that they are not part of the political world which they study. Political theory must break with the practical preoccupations of the classical thinkers, otherwise there is no possibility that traditional muddles, contradictory hypotheses and conceptual culs-de-sac can ever be sorted out. Theorising is an activity which is at one remove from the real world. Instead of analysing words, behaviouralists restrict their analysis to external and empirically accessible facts, but in practice they come to the same conclusions as the linguistic philosophers.

Both the linguistic philosophers and the behaviouralists argue therefore that while concepts like state, power and democracy are contestable in the real world, there is no reason why an academic analysis of these concepts needs to be similarly partisan and controversial in character. It is both possible and desirable to construct political theories which have no implications for political practice. But is it?

Linguistic analysts accept that they must do more than merely record the way in which people use words. They are after all philosophers and not merely philologists. They have to adjudicate on what is the *correct* use of words, but how is this possible without expressing a preference for one usage over another? When linguistic philosophers, for example, analyse the word 'democracy' or the word 'freedom', they can argue for one usage only by arguing against others. To contend, say, that the concept of democracy ought to apply to participatory rather than representative systems of government, or that the term 'freedom' is best understood positively as 'freedom to', rather than negatively as 'freedom from', means taking sides in an ongoing debate. Participatory democrats are critical of hierarchy; representative democrats more readily accept it. The advocates of positive freedom usually favour egalitarianism; the supporters of negative liberty generally oppose it. How then can the meaning or use of words be divorced from a debate about their content?

Miller explores the possibility of adopting a 'half-way house' position in which linguistic analysts merely specify a 'permissible' use of words, as opposed to a use of words which they actually prefer. But he has to conclude (1983, p. 51) that even here the criteria chosen to determine which usage is 'permissible' and which is not will still of necessity betray a practical bias (see also Hall and Madood, 1979, p. 343). The only way to avoid taking sides is to stop analysing concepts altogether.

A similar difficulty confronts the behaviouralists. No behaviouralist can investigate, for example, the question of apathy in politics, or the role of elites in a democracy, without coming up against what might be called the 'functionality' problem. Do these phenomena help or hinder the running of society? Whether something is functional or dysfunctional for society is part and parcel of what it is. At the same time it is impossible to identify a phenomenon as functional or dysfunctional without at the same time revealing an obvious political standpoint. The argument that, for example, apathy enables a society to function more smoothly, or that elites serve to entrench rather than undermine democratic values, cannot but have implications for practical politics.

These difficulties all stem from the fact that linguistic philosophers and behavioural political scientists are unable to tackle a question which ought to be crucial to their argument, but which they make it impossible for themselves to answer. Why theories at all? Why theorise more in some situations than in others? Why theorise in different ways at different times? This is a question upon which the classical political tradition throws a fascinating light.

Whether we think of Plato or Hobbes, Burke or Rousseau, Marx or Mill, the classical political theorists all theorised because they believed that society was confronted with major practical problems which could not be solved without sustained political thought. Improving theory was a way of improving practice. Plato (1955, p. 14) took the view that once true philosophers obtained power, the affairs of society and the individual could be justly regulated. Hobbes hoped that his speculative writings about politics would be 'converted' into 'the Utility of Practice' (1968, p. 408), while Rousseau believed that he had found a way of making governments legitimate. It is true that Burke feared the practical consequences of speculative theory, but it is precisely because he *shared* the classical view of political theory as a response to practical crisis that he considered it a sure sign of an ill-conducted state that its people resort to political theories. The less theory we need the better! Mill assiduously polished his essay *On Liberty* in order to maximise its public impact, while Marx obviously thought that sound revolutionary theory was of great practical relevance. The classical thinkers, however much they disagreed on other matters, all took the view that political theory is necessarily related to political practice.

The linkage between the two is further borne out, if we ask another question: why was is that in the 1950s and 1960s British and American political theorists did think that it was possible to stand outside of the world of politics in an apparently detached and disinterested way. Linguistic philosophers argued that traditional political theory was 'dead', while behaviouralists generally subscribed to the 'end of ideology' thesis. For, as Partridge (1967) pointed out at the time, this contention was itself the product of political consensus, and it was not only the academics who thought that partisanship was a bad thing—so too did the politicians! The attempt to restrict theory to language analysis or to the 'value-free' testing of empirical data was itself a particular response to (a perceived lack of) practical problems. This is not to say that using words carefully or testing empirical data rigorously are purely trivial or unimportant aspects of serious scholarship. Rather the point is that a widely held belief that crisis and turmoil had disappeared from the Western world created the *illusion* that theory without practice is possible: that political theorists can somehow theorise about politics in a non-political way.

It is revealing therefore that as the future of the post-war world becomes clouded with uncertainty, and consensus politics crumbles, so normative theory of a traditional kind has revived, and linguistic philsophy and behaviouralism lost ground. Today the relationship between political theory and political practice is much more obvious than it was a decade and a half ago. We can now see more clearly why the very attempt to divorce theory from practice is itself a political response to practical circumstances.

IS POLITICAL THEORY NECESSARILY IDEOLOGICAL?

Some behaviouralists have conceded that in their enthusiastic quest for methodological purity they may have unwittingly purveyed 'an ideology of social conservatism tempered by modest incremental change' (Easton, 1971a, p. 326). But even if we accept that political theory has practical implications and consequences, does this mean therefore that it is ideological in character? A number of political theorists vigorously dissent from such a view. Yet, they concede, political theory may be normative and prescriptive: but ideological? Never!

A number of points are adduced to support this argument. Political theory, it is said, must be committed to knowledge for its own sake. It cannot countenance in the way ideology does the use of ideas as polemical instruments to advance particular interests in everyday life. Yet the classical thinkers (even before Marx) did not see theory as irrelevant to everyday needs. If they were less concerned to respond to immediate problems, this was because they believed that the problems facing society were so deeply rooted that only a profound theoretical analysis could sort them out.

Political theory, it is argued, must be expounded in an open-minded and balanced way, while ideologies veer towards intolerant and illiberal extremism. Political theorists are committed to moderation, ideologists to a totalitarian radical-ism. But if moderate circumstances require moderate responses, why shouldn't extreme problems necessitate solutions of a thorough-going kind? Those who think that changing society 'as a whole' implies some kind of sinister 'totalitarian' project make the equally 'totalitarian' assumption that the basic structures of society are generally sound (Hughes, 1966, p. 185). Are we to judge Plato as unbalanced and 'extremist' just because he was *profoundly* conservative, or imagine Hobbes to be an intolerant fanatic when a good case can be made for regarding the 'radical' author of the *Leviathan* as the founder of modern liberalism?

Ideologies, we are told, lack critical judgment and rational justification. Hence they violate the canons of acceptable political theorising. It is true that radical ideologies can be irrational and unthinking, but an absence of critical scholarship is not the monopoly of theoretical radicals. Indeed it could well be argued that it is the critics of ideology who lack critical awareness, since they seem oblivious to that world of subterranean assumptions which underpins consensus theory. Moderates (particularly of a Burkean variety) have after all been known to extol the practical virtues of unthinking prejudice and irrational custom. As with the arguments of the behaviouralists and the linguistic philosophers, it has to be said that these criticisms of ideology are themselves open to serious objection.

Once we accept that political theory arises as a response to political practice, then there seems to be no good reason to deny its ideological character. But because political theory is necessarily linked to political practice, does this mean that its expositions are indistinguishable from the work of party propagandists and political publicists who (as we noted at the outset) *also* make use of political concepts? It is this point above all which makes so many political theorists (Horton, 1984, p. 119 is a recent example) anxious to differentiate political theory from what they call 'ideological' thought.

Here it would seem appropriate to introduce the major methodological postulate which underlies the basic argumentation of this book. I shall call this postulate (less it appear too commonplace and undistinguished) Hoffman's *First Law of Philosophical Obscurantism*. It states: things (whether conceptual or real) can be distinguished from one another only because they have something in common, and they can be the same only when they are also different. Everything unites through distinction, and can be distinguished only through unity.

To tackle the problem at hand. Both political theory and party propaganda are tied to political practice. Hence they are, in the sense, the 'same' or at least, similar. But it does not follow from this that they cannot also be distinguished. Three important differences can be noted without any difficulty.

Firstly the audience which the two address is different. Party propagandists are concerned with the public in general and their prospective supporters in particular (Wood, 1978). Political theorists, on the other hand, generally write for a (regrettably) smaller group of individuals who are either academically trained, or who are anxious to educate themselves in a serious and systematic way. Secondly the style of argument is different. Political theorists must strictly adhere to the canons of scholarship so that rhetoric is curtailed in favour of logic, and sober evidence advanced in place of extravagant emotion. This points to a third difference.

It is not the task of the political theorist to exhort people to undertake a particular course of action at a particular time and a particular place. Thinking about a problem is crucial to solving it, but it is not the same as actually organising people to implement the solution. Political theorists must therefore be distinguishable from practical politicians, even though they may of course also adopt this role as well.

But these differences should not allow us to overlook the similarities. Political theory is still related to political practice in its own academic way, and must therefore (like works of party propaganda) be controversial and 'contestable' in character. The contestability of political theory does not erode its academic standing although, on this point, there is uncertainty and confusion even among those who defend the 'contestability' thesis.

Some have asserted (Gallie, 1955, pp 188–93) that while political concepts (like democracy or freedom) are essentially contestable, we have no way of resolving the respective merits of competing arguments. We can note the rival justifications offered (they are more than mere emotional outpourings), but we cannot evaluate them in terms of a general principle which commands ultimate agreement.

Yet this argument is curiously defeatist and relativistic in implication. For what is the point of declaring political concepts 'contestable' if we have no way of identifying winners and losers in the 'contest'? Why note rival definitions of democracy or freedom if we cannot at the same time justify the one we prefer? This version of the 'contestability thesis' may seem at variance with linguistic and behaviouralist positions, but in practice it allows a similar kind of 'positivism' to slip in through the back door. Contestable political theory cannot remain a serious enterprise unless we can make the kind of judgments about contentious concepts which enables us to expound one in preference to another.

Academic political theory, in other words, can still be *political* theory while remaining strictly academic. Like all forms of political theory, it is a response to the world of practice. Hence it is necessarily ideological, but in its own distictively academic way. Distinctions should not be turned into 'disjunctions' (Parekh, 1968, pp. 181–2); we should avoid constructing rigid barriers between interpenetrating concepts.

Indeed one practical point which flows from this argument is that the relationship between academic theory and everyday political propaganda and publicist writing can (and should) be a mutually enhancing one, despite the differences involved.

Academic theory raises the tone and quality of public debate when good causes are strengthened by good arguments, while party propaganda and publicist pamphleteering can provide challenging points of reference which help to make academic theory more relevant and useful. Diminishing the differences may yield benefits to theory and practice alike.

A book about the state, power and democracy is thus of necessity both a work of political theory and a contribution to political debate. Although, as we have seen, academic political theorists are not practising politicians, it is still possible and permissible to identify their writing with 'soft' political labels in a way which acknowledges partisanship while respecting academic character. Hence in this work we will encounter with varying frequency ideologists of the Old and the New Left; the Old and New Right, and a number of groupings in the centre whom it is tempting to classify as Consensus Liberals and Apolitical Moderates.

Given the conceptual centrality of state, power and democracy to contemporary political debate, this book, like all textbooks on politics, is a political work in its own right. Axes will inevitably be ground, but (hopefully) with a scholarly restraint. This means that readers must discover for themselves the author's own particular allegiances and the book's overall ideological hue.

PART ONE
STATE AND POLITICS

1 The Problem of the State

A CONTESTABLE CONCEPT?

Part One seeks to establish the identity of the state, and sets out to do so by relating the question of the state to the concept of politics. Linking the state to politics in this way reflects a wider commitment to the idea that concepts are always best grasped in relationship to one another, and we have already argued in the introduction that 'state, power and democracy' form a 'contentious triad of contestable concepts' in which each throws light on the others. The same also holds for the concepts individually. Each can best be understood when analysed in relationship to a conceptual partner with whom it enjoys a central but troubled affinity. The choice of partner is intended to highlight the contestability of the concept, and thus to locate its involvement in current controversy.

With these criteria in mind, we propose the following 'partnerships': the state in relationship to politics; power in relationship to authority; and democracy in relation to liberalism. In each case, as we shall see, the conceptual partner chosen helps to focus and structure argument by providing a useful practical link with issues currently being debated in the everyday political world.

The concept of the state is a surprisingly contentious one. It is not difficult to see why the relationship between democracy and liberalism should be contestable—given the contradictory way in which democracy is defined in practical politics—and argument has long raged over the problem of force and morality in the analysis of power and authority. But why should the concept of the state be controversial?

True, an anarchist would like the state abolished. A Marxist wants the state to disappear. A liberal would have its powers restricted, while a conservative might extol its sovereign acts of force. But why should there be any disagreement about the importance of the state as a concept in political theory? 'Authoritarians' and 'anarchists' alike can surely agree that the state is central to understanding politics. Yet a striking feature of post-war political science has been the lack of interest in the concept of the state, and even more than this, a widespread rejection of its utility as a theoretical concept.

It is true that scepticism about the conceptual value of the state can be found before the Second World War, and Bernard Crick has argued that American political science traditionally focused on social institutions rather than the state as such (1959, p. 30; p. 96). Bentley's (characteristically American) 'process' view of politics, in which the state is simply regarded as one 'government' among many (1967, p. 263; p. 300), was first published in 1908. Yet it remains true that until the 1940s and 1950s conceptual anti-statism was not influential, and it was widely held that the study of politics begins and ends with the state.

Why then has the state become controversial even as a concept in political theory? Challenging it for conceptual supremacy is sometimes 'government' (as in Bentley's analysis), but more typically it has been the 'political system' or just 'politics'. A state-centred theory, it is argued, is narrow and limiting: politics can be much more profitably identified as taking place within a multiplicity of social relationships. The state is simply one kind of politics—different in degree but not in kind— and it does not deserve any special status in the theoretical world.

This is the argument which we shall tackle in the course of this chapter.

THE STATE AND THE POLITICS OF PROBLEMS

Why should post-war political theory have downgraded the concept of the state? It is at least worthy of comment that many of those who have argued that the the state has no special significance in the study of politics have *also* taken the position, as noted in the introduction, that political theory ought to be radically divorced from political practice.

Linguistic philosophers like T.D. Weldon dispute the contention that the state is qualitatively different from other social institutions (1953, pp. 46–7). Behaviouralists build upon Arthur Bentley's earlier arguments, asserting that the state is too ideological and restrictive to be helpful as an organising concept in political theory. As a result of both these onslaughts, the state has, as one writer puts it, been 'withering away' in the face of 'political authority', the 'political system', 'administration' and 'society' for the past thirty years (Mann, 1980, p. 296).

All this raises an intriguing question. If behaviouralists and linguistic philosophers reject *both* the centrality of the state and the practical relevance of political theory, is there not perhaps a connection between these two positions? Why should those who seek a 'pure' political theory also wish to de-emphasise the significance of the state? It is true that some radical theorists who favour a practical political theory also support a non-statist view of politics, and we will examine the logic of their position later. For the moment, however, it is important to explore the linkage between the 'consensus liberalism' of the behaviouralists and the linguistic philosophers, on the one hand, and their repudiation of the state as a key concept in political thought, on the other.

We can begin to make sense of this linkage if we recall the emphasis placed by the classical political tradition upon the importance of theory as a way of tackling practical problems. In Plato's *Republic*, for example, the political philosopher can heal society's woes only if society is restructured through the medium of a radically different kind of *state* or, as Plato called it, a 'polis'. We will leave until later the question as to how ancient, medieval and modern concepts of the state relate to one another.

As far as Plato is concerned, it is precisely because problems in society are so deeply rooted that an institution like the state is required to resolve them—an association which, in Aristotle's view, stands supreme over all others (1962, p. 25). A

Leviathan, says Hobbes, is needed to tackle humanity's problems, for, as he sees it, society will dissolve into universal chaos unless the sovereign majesty of the state can create the basis for universal order. 'Everything', Rousseau declares, 'is rooted in politics': no people can be other than their government has made them (1953, p. 377). Where a people are born free but are everywhere in chains, only an institution embodying the principles of political right can create legitimacy. This classical preoccupation with what we would today call the state, was premissed on the assumption that existing social conditions are profoundly unsatisfactory. The very university of the state's jurisdiction is called into play by the breadth and the scope of the problems which it has to sort out.

It is revealing therefore that contemporary theorists who see a significant role for the state also stress the importance of practically oriented political theory, even though they may agree about little else. A New Left writer like Ralph Miliband deplores the lack of interest in the state by academic theorists in the 1950s and 1960s, and ascribes this 'remarkable paradox' to the complacency of the Consensus Liberals (1973, p. 4). An analyst of the New Right like Norman Barry finds the dearth of books and articles about the state 'surprising', and observes that arguments about the state cannot be understood without reference to 'evaluative political principles in general' (1981, p. 46–7). Boith endorse our linkage argument. Deny a role for value judgments in political theory, and the peculiar importance of the state as an 'association of associations' ceases to be (as linguistic analysts would say) 'philosophically interesting'.

A politics of problems requires the conceptual focus of the state. Nozick's 'minimal' liberal polity (1974) has little in common with Fydor Burlatksy's Soviet political system (1978); yet each theorist structures his political analysis around the state. Marxists and classically minded liberals can both stress the conceptual importance of state sovereignty while radically disagreeing over its relationship to the class structure of society. What unites all 'statists', past and present, is a common adherence to the evaluative and normative role of political theory as conceived in the classical tradition.

Indeed this relationship between a focus on the state and a practical conception of political theory is borne out in a most revealing way if we compare the positions of two leading behavioural political theorists. Both subscribe to the view that politics is best analysed as a 'system' rather than in terms of the state, and both argue that a 'scientific' political theory ought to be 'purely' empirical and value free in character. But even more interesting than the similarities are the differences, and the light these differences throw on the argument which I have advanced in this chapter.

Robert Dahl defines politics as any persistent pattern of human relationships that involves, to any significant extent, control, influence, power or authority (1976, p. 3). Politics is to be found in virtually every human association, at every level in society. All political systems have governments, he argues, and the 'Government' (i.e. the state) is just one government among many. Dahl does accept a Weberian definition of the state as a government which claims to exclusively regulate the legitimate use of force within a given territorial area. But he remains sceptical about the merits of 'dichotomous definitions' (i.e. those which focus on a monopoly or concentration of power), and gives the state or 'Government' no special place in his political analysis.

Although behavioural like Dahl's in its general orientation, David Easton's 'systems analysis' differs significantly in its details. Whereas Dahl is sympathetic to the view of politics as the study of power, Easton finds this conception too broad, and proposes instead to confine the term 'political' to specifically *public* matters. Politics, he argues, is best defined as an authoritative allocation of values which regulates not the existence of any particular group within society, but the life of society as a whole (1953, p. 134). Politics arises, in other words, when the *private* arbitration of disputes fails, and a public agency has to intervene.

Dahl is sceptical. In an early review of Easton's first major work, *The Political System*, he sharply criticises this 'holistic' concept of politics. Easton's distinction between the authoritative allocation of values for society as a whole—'whatever that means' (1954-5, p. 481)—and the allocation of values for lesser associations is a false and arbitrary one, for it is an analysis,

Dahl argues, which cannot be tested in empirical terms. We shall return later to this and other criticisms of Easton's definition, but for the moment it is worth noting that Easton's stress upon a public and holistic view of politics is accompanied by an agonised and tortuous discussion on the role of political theory as a response to social problems.

Whereas Dahl simply takes the view that empirical theory must be value free, Easton argues that the subject matter of political science is 'central to the solution of our present social crisis'. He praises the 'critical inclinations of the Greeks' (1953, p. 3; p. 43), and devotes a whole chapter of *The Political System* to what he calls 'the moral foundations of theoretical research'. On the other hand, he continues to accept an essentially positivist view of values as emotional responses (1953, p. 221).

When he returns to the question some twenty years later to argue that the task of 'creative moral inquiry' is even more urgent than it was before, he reaffirms the traditional behaviouralist position that empirical analysis should not be confused with moral theorising (1971b, pp. 363–4). In other words Easton still subscribes to the view that empirical theory in itself is pure and 'non-practical', and he remains militantly opposed to the concept of the state as a respectable instrument of theoretical research (1981, p. 306).

Easton is, however, a behaviouralist with an uneasy conscience. He is anxious to take account of moral problems, even if he is unable to find a way of coherently tackling them. This is why his view of politics is more holistic and publicly oriented than Dahl's, since it is clear to Easton that society 'as a whole' continues to have serious and unresolved problems confronting it. His concern about morality is reflected in a view of politics that is much close to the 'critical inclinations of the Greeks'.

There is then an important link between a statist and a problem-oriented view of political theory. Nevertheless it has to be said that establishing the existence of such a link does not in itself justify placing the state at the centre of politics. Indeed there are those who strongly support a practical role for political theory, and yet with equal passion *reject* the statist conception. Any attempt to restrict political analysis to a study of the state, they argue, reflects an elitist desire to discourage social-wide participation in the political process, and this argument even leads one radical critic (Skillen, 1977, pp. 22–3) to insist that Dahl and Easton must be full-blown statists, since as 'establishment theorists' they are apparently not in favour of mass, participatory politics from below!

We need to take account therefore of a radical as well as a conservative anti-statism, and my arguments here apply only to the latter tradition as it has expressed itself through the linguistic and behaviouralist positions of the post-war period. Radical anti-statists (and we will return to their contentions later) believe that political theory ought consciously to assist political practice, and that the 'wider' the conception of politics, the more democratic and radical this practice will be (Leftwich, 1984, p. 11).

The question then of whether a state-centred view of politics is justified cannot simply be resolved through an argument over the relationship between political theory and practice. True, a purist rejection of practice helps to explain a conceptual rejection of the state; but even if *all* anti-statists agreed that political theory ought to be non-evaluative and ethically neutral, this in itself would still not dispose of the question as to whether politics ought to be conceptualised in terms of the state.

The case for and against state-centred theory must be viewed on its own merits. This point is worth emphasising since, as we shall now see, the objections which can be raised against defining politics in terms of the state are powerful ones, even if (in the last analysis) they are by no means overwhelming.

THE STATE AND THE PROBLEM OF POLITICS

Those who challenge the centrality of the state to political theory invariably embrace some version of what I shall call the 'breadth argument'—the argument that focussing on the state excludes from the realm of politics whole areas of social activity which ought to be included.

The breadth argument can be broadly summarised as

follows. It is a matter of record that the term 'state' first appears in the sixteenth century when it is employed (by Machiavelli, for example,) as a conceptual counterweight to the internecine struggles between Pope and Emperor, monarch and lord. Historically, in other words, the concept arose as an ideological tool used to justify the centralising policies of the absolute monarch. Statists place themselves in the absurd position of implying that because there was no state (in the modern sense of the term) before the seventeenth century, there was therefore no politics.

Even if we accept, so the argument continues, that the ancient and medieval world did possess some kind of state, what are we to say of tribal societies where no institution capable of monopolising legitimate force on a territorial basis can be found at all? What of the international area? If politics is to be defined as an activity which centres on the state, are diplomatic negotiations and international treaties simply a form of 'anarchy', and hence, like tribal societies, beyond the scope of political study? Take the question of the family, trade unions, schools, churches, multi-national corporations and many other social bodies: are these institutions non-political in character merely because they are not (at least normally) regarded as part of the state? Surely it is unjustifiably restrictive to exclude them from theoretical consideration as the result of a statist conception of the political process.

The breadth argument is an important one, but it has to be said that some of its objections are weightier than others. The contention that the concept of the state is too burdened with the practical overtones of 'statecraft' and its 'ideological' need to justify sovereign power, is not one which need detain us, since we have already challenged the view that political theory can be divorced from political practice. There is therefore no reason to suppose that concepts used in preference to the state, like 'political system' or 'government', will be any less contestable or ideologically charged in character.

But what of the argument that because the term 'state' is used in its modern sense only from the end of the medieval period, it follows that before the seventeenth century (broadly speaking), there was no state at all. Although this contention is advanced by a number of serious scholars (Easton, 1953, p.

109; Parekh, 1968, p. 158), most political theorists reject it. They take the view that while there are undoubtedly important differences between the modern state, the ancient Greek *polis*, the Roman republic and the medieval kingdom, there is nevertheless an important 'something' which they all have in common as institutions concentrating power in the hands of clearly identifiable rulers.

It is true that the Greek city states were small, exclusive concerns, combining territorially based coercion with morally integrative functions. They had no developed sense of 'separation' between church and state or state and society. The Roman republic, on the other hand, had a clearer idea of a distinct public realm but it was more strictly defined by law than by territoriality (Hall, 1984a, p. 3). The feudal kingdom was highly fragmented, and in the middle ages different words were used to describe different aspects of the system, whether *regnum* as the territorial monarchy, *respublica* as the wider community based on church and empire, and *civitas* as the city state or commune that flourished in places like Italy (D'Entreves, 1967, p. 29).

We can readily concede therefore that with the rise of a new and unifying term—the 'state'—there was also the development of a more unified and absolutist rule. Power was more explicitly gathered up under a single sovereign head. The modern state, it might be said, is rather more 'state-like' than its predecessors. It conforms more precisely to the general definition of the state as an institution monopolising legitimate force, but it does not follow from this that institutions concentrating power in a less unified way, or with a less clearly differentiated public realm, are not still states. It is true, as Max Weber says, that the concept of the state 'has only in modern times reached its full development' (1964, p. 156). But these less developed institutions still had *pretensions* to sovereignty (even where this was bitterly contested between king and emperor), and they invested 'legitimate force' in the hands of rulers who enjoyed a proceduralised power of life and death over their subjects.

It might be objected that in these earlier 'states' this monopoly of legitimate force was rather formal and deceptive, and that its legitimacy was problematic given the despotic nature of the rule. Forsyth (1987, p. 586) has recently argued that while we can speak of these earlier polities as states, they were too divided to possess 'sovereignty'. But, as we shall soon see, it is not only pre-modern states which have problems of formality and deception, sovereignty, contested legitimacy and an ambiguous divide between the public and the private. These problems are inherent in *all* states, past and present.

The argument therefore that the state did not exist before the modern period is not really tenable. There is no good reason to believe that a state-centred theory of politics need to be *this* restrictive in its scope and application. But this still leaves other aspects of the breadth argument to be tackled, and here the objections are rather more substantial in character.

THE BREADTH ARGUMENT VS. THE IDENTITY PROBLEM

The proponents of the breadth argument note the fact that humans have lived most of their history in societies without a state. Yet, they protest, the supporters of a state-centred theory of politics would appear to deny the relevance of these stateless orders to an understanding of political theory.

Moreover, statists would also seem to want to exclude international agencies and relationships from political consideration, and seek to 'depoliticise' the conflicts taking place in social institutions like the family, the trade union, the school and the business corporation. D.D. Raphael might contend (1976, p. 30) that these struggles are 'political' only in a 'metaphoric' and 'parasitic' sense of the term, but who can deny that these 'broader' social institutions make a significant impact on the way the state itself functions? Surely, the champions of the breadth argument conclude, the statist view is not only parochial, but it is one which invites an uncritical view of the state itself.

The broad social definition emphasises by way of contrast the ubiquitous character of the political process so that, as Dahl puts it, 'almost every human association has its political aspect' (1976, p. 3). On the face of it, the breadth argument is an appealing one, but what may appear conceptually attractive is not necessarily logically sound. A moment's reflection suggests that the broader the definition of politics, the more difficult it is to say what politics really is. After all if politics is ubiquitous, i.e. virtually synonymous with all other human activity, how can we locate its *distinctive* identity?

Adrian Leftwich's definition of politics exemplifies the problem. It is so catholic in its scope that it is worth quoting verbatim. Politics, Leftwich tells us, 'consists of all activities of cooperation and conflict, within and between societies, whereby the human species goes about obtaining, using, producing and distributing resources in the course of the pro-duction and the reproduction of its social and biological life' (1983, p. 11). This makes my point. If politics consists, as Left-which says, of *all* the activities of co-operation and conflict in the production and reproduction of social life, what does it exclude? Politics ceases to be just one 'aspect' of a human association (as Dahl insists), and becomes merely another word for human activity itself.

Indeed Leftwich seems to accept this point when he says that 'politics is central to the life of the human species' (1983, p. 26). Choosing to spend your pocket money in one way rather than another is just as political as enacting a law or overthrowing a state. The conventional distinctions between sociology, economics, politics, psychology (even biology?) all dissolve, and at least in terms of the human sciences, politics is every-thing and everywhere. The breadth argument appears to run blindly into an identity crisis.

This is a problem which puts most proponents of the broad definition of politics onto the defensive, whether they are Con-sensus Liberals and Apolitical Moderates of the behavioural school, or left-wing radicals. Take, as a particularly interesting example of the latter, the way in which this question arises in the work of Antonio Gramsci. Gramsci was impressed by Benedetto Croce's broad 'practical' view of politics, which seeks to dissolve the particular features of the state into the 'dynamic' processes of life in general. Following one of the frequent discussions he has on Croce's ideas in *The Prison Notebooks*, Gramsci poses the question: 'In what sense can one identify politics with history, and hence all of life with politics?' (1971, p. 137).

His response to this question is equivocal. On the one hand, he seems anxious to identify politics specifically, and to distinguish it in particular from economics. This is why he expresses his dissatisfaction with Croce's view of politics as passion. On the other hand, his own view of politics is so broad—he defines it as an impulse to action which becomes permanent (1971, pp. 137–8)—that it is difficult to see how it can be distinguished from economics or indeed any other social activity. Elsewhere in *The Prison Notebooks* Gramsci tells us that people are 'political beings' because they modify the environment in which they develop, establishing norms of conduct in the process (1971, p. 265). But if this is so, then politics is still a synonym for social life in general, and the problem of locating its *specific* attributes remains unresolved.

This is a question which particularly bothers Dahl. Though a 'broad' theorist, Dahl is acutely conscious of the need to distinguish politics as just *one* aspect among many within human associations (1976, p. 4). After all, if political theory involves analysing behaviour, then it must be able to analyse its own distinctive identity as well. Dahl's contention, we recall, is that politics focusses upon power, control, influence or authority. Psychology, economics, sociology, etc. all study *other* aspects of human behaviour. But how are we to distinguish them?

Take Dahl's view that economics, unlike politics, is concerned with scarce resources and the production and distribution of goods and services. Yet given the fact that the production and distribution of scarce resources also generate problems of power and authority (this point is made clearly enough in Leftwich's definition), how meaningful is this distinction? Dahl himself defines capitalism, for example, as an *economic* system in which productive activities are privately owned and controlled. The word 'control' appears both in the definition of politics and in his definition of economics, and Dahl would find it hard to deny that economic relationships under capitalism also involve questions of power, influence and authority as well.

Indeed he explicitly concedes this point in his recent book *A Preface to Economic Democracy*, where he argues that a private business can be viewed as a political system in which relations of power exist between government and governed, and that crucial political inequalities originate in the ownership and control of corporate capitalist firms (1985, p. 85; p. 4). This admission serves to further underline the difficulty which political theorists face in trying to distinguish politics from economics (or indeed from any other social activity), when a broad, non-statist view of the subject is employed.

Yet what of David Easton's non-statist attempt (which we have already encountered) to identify politics as the authoritative allocation of values for society as a whole? Easton considers but rejects broad power-oriented definitions of the kind favoured by Dahl, and he does so precisely because of the problems of identity they create. If the power relations of a gang, family or church group are as political as the activities of parties or legislatures, then, as Easton notes, what we have is the identification of political science with social science in general, and no coherent basis exists for distinguishing politics from other areas of social research (1953, p. 101).

Hence Easton argues for a definition of politics as the authoritative allocation of values for society as a whole. Values may well be authoritatively allocated in all kinds of social organisations—from trade unions to the church—but these allocations only become *political* in character when institutions cannot settle their problems informally and in private. An agency whose scope covers all of society's activities and tasks, has to intervene (1953, pp. 136–7). The social-wide focus of its authoritative allocations endows the political system with that public quality which sets it apart from the economic, cultural and other aspects of social life. This is what gives politics 'its minimal homogeneity and cohesion' (1953, p. 134).

Undoubtedly, this is a definition which appears to succeed admirably in differentiating the political system from the rest of society. But, as Easton's reviewers and commentators have been quick to ask, how does it actually differentiate politics from the *state*? Surely it is precisely the existence of an 'allocative' mechanism able to enforce decisions for society as a whole which constitutes the state's most distinctive attribute. It is difficult not to conlcude therefore that in rejecting a power-based definition of politics in favour of a holistic one,

Easton has simply allowed the concept of the state to creep in through the back door.

Easton is of course willing to concede that the state itself functions as a political system in its own right—authoritatively allocating values for society as a whole. But, he insists, stateless societies also have mechanisms which function in this way. So does the international community. Thus Easton tells us that the strife within a migratory tribe for the control of its resources is 'exactly similar' to what we would consider political struggle (1953, p. 111), while at the other end of the 'size' spectrum, the UN and the League of Nations are good examples of political systems authoritatively allocating values from a society which is international in its scope. We must, Easton argues, get away from the 'statist' prejudice that the allocative mechanisms of a political system necessarily involve formal or rational procedures. In fact, violent conflict between states or the secession of one clan from the rest of the tribe may also constitute mechanisms for implementing authoritative policy (1953, p. 141).

This rather ingenious argument throws us back, however, onto Easton's initial definition. If values can be authoritatively allocated through tribal secession or international conflict, in what sense can we speak of their allocation for a society 'as a whole'? After all Easton defines society as a 'special kind of human grouping' in which people develop a 'sense of belonging together' (1953, p. 135). Secession or war would seem to indicate not the presence but indeed the *absence* of society as Easton himself defines it. To argue therefore that values can be authoritatively allocated for society as a whole when this society is being torn apart either by war or secession seems very odd, to say the least.

This problem emerges most acutely in Easton's attempt to build into his systems analysis an element of dynamism. Anxious to defend his model from the charge that it betrays a conservative and functionalist bias, Easton introduces the concept of a political system 'persisting through change'. This makes it possible, he suggests, for a system to continue authoritatively allocating values while its structures dramatically alter as it does so. Thus it can be said, for example, that a political system persisted in Germany even though the imperial order fell to the Weimar Republic, which in turn yielded to the Nazi regime, only to be succeeded by a very different order after the Second World War (1965, p. 83).

But if this is so, then both the society and the 'persisting' political system become hopelessly problematic as a result. After all post-war Germany, following its earlier upheavals, actually divided into two sharply differentiated societies with two (statist) political systems of a strikingly variant character. Can it be seriously supposed that above and beyond these 'natural' political systems, some kind of shadowy 'analytical' political system continued allocating values for what had now become a highly abstract 'society as a whole'? Indeed, if *this* is what Easton means by political activities, then, as one reviewer acidly comments, it is hard to see what could change a political system short of some kind of catastrophe which physically obliterates all its popular participants (Converse, 1965, pp. 1061–2).

Easton, in other words, can rescue his argument from a 'statist' bias only by constructing a ghostly analytical mechanism capable of authoritatively allocating values in a transcendental world beyond and above historical and social reality. Once the model's creator returns to earth in order to try to identify a *real* political system, he comes face to face with the unpalatable fact that the only mechanism actually capable of resolving conflict for society 'as a whole' is his old *bête noire*, the state.

The truth is, to return to our two examples of non-statist 'political systems', that stateless societies simply dissolve when the conflicts which divide them cannot be resolved through informal social pressures, and the international community can maintain its social cohesion only when states abstain from 'sovereign' acts of war. Easton has made therefore, despite strenuous efforts to the contrary, a compelling case for the state's centrality in a theory of politics. As long as disputes cannot be privately settled without the coercive intervention of an authoritative public agency from on high, society will require a *state*. Easton has succeeded in locating the specific and distinctive character of the political process only by highlighting the state's importance.

It may well be, as we have already hinted, that the state is a rather curious institution. It does, on the face of it, seem odd to speak of an institution authoritatively allocating values for society 'as a whole' because that society is too *divided* to settle its differences in a purely social manner. But this, we must insist, is not simply a conceptual problem. It is a problem with the state itself, and seeking to replace the state with some other concept can do nothing, as the fate of Easton's own 'political system' shows, to resolve the contradictory and paradoxical character of the political process.

Our problem then is this. Cogent objections can undoubtedly be raised against a state-centred theory of politics, and yet once we move beyond the state in our search for a definition, the breadth argument, as we have called it, is rapidly destabilised by an identity crisis. Either we have what appears on the surface to be a narrow and restrictive concept of politics, or we have no coherent concept at all. Either dissolve politics into society—or stick with the state! That seems to be the choice which confronts us.

THE STATE AND THE PROBLEM OF ORIGINS

It is perfectly true that one *can* defend a state-centred theory of politics by arguing that stateless societies are of no interest to political theory, and that only societies which are 'sophisticated' or 'civilised' enough to have states deserve our attention.

Indeed many statists take this position. According to Raphael, we can largely ignore societies without a state since the problems of political philosophy arise only in communities where there are 'sophisticated ideas' (1976, p. 29). We should confine our attention to 'advanced and complex' societies with states because it is only through a state-centred process of politics that 'genuine freedom' arises (Crick, 1982, p. 17). In fact, Hegel even advances the argument that stateless societies not only lack freedom but rationality as well, so that it is quite impossible anyway to really understand them. Filled with 'revolutions, nomadic wanderings and the strangest mutations', these societies are destitute of an objective history because without a literate ruling class, they have no 'subjective history' (1956, p. 61). The stateless world is not just philosophically uninteresting: it is theoretically unintelligible because it takes the reality of the state to make the world meaningful in the first place.

Yet does it really follow as the logical consequence of a state-centred theory of politics that we have to ignore the reality of stateless societies? Indeed the first thing that has to be said about this line of argument is that it is extremely complacent. Is it really true that 'advanced and complex' statist societies are self-evidently more 'sophisticated' than 'primitive' stateless ones? We wonder, and certainly Rousseau did when in his justly celebrated *Discourses* he emphasised the corrupting consequences of 'civilisation'.

Rousseau was concerned not with a return to a 'state of nature' but rather to demonstrate the awesome price which humanity has paid for its 'progress'. The leisure necessary to cultivate the arts and sciences was, he observed, made possible only through social inequality and the institution of slavery. The accumulation of wealth has been accompanied by misery and poverty. Public moralising has developed hand in hand with the private corruption of virtue. Our highly prized individualism has simply enabled us to close our eyes and ears to the sufferings of others. Property has spawned 'crimes, wars and murders' (1973, p. 76), while our much vaunted 'reason' has merely given us the facility to spin the 'sophisticated' webs of deception necessary to justify cynically a divided society. As for the birth of the state—that rational embodiment of our universal freedom—this was an event in which 'all ran headlong to their chains'. For the 'advantage of a few ambitious individuals', humanity subjected itself to 'perpetual labour, slavery and wretchedness' (1973, p. 89).

This blistering attack on the complacent arguments of an uncritical statism prompts the following thought. If the state is the kind of unqualified blessing to humanity which some statists suppose, why is it that humanity today stands menaced by the threat of extermination through nuclear war? There can be little doubt, as Miliband (1973, p. 3) has reminded us, that should part of our planet be laid to nuclear waste, it will be because people, acting in the name of the state and invested with its power, will have so decided.

But the belief that stateless societies are unsophisticated, uncivilised and of no interest to political theory, is not only complacent. It is, particularly in its Hegelian formulation, also thoroughly mystical, since if stateless societies are uninteresting and unintelligible to us, then how is the birth of the state itself to be rationally explained? We have a logical problem here as well as a moral one. If stateless societies lacked coherent development, then how did the state itself with all its majestic freedom and rationality arise? It is all very well for Hegel to say grandly that the state created its history and development through 'the very progress of its own being' (1956, p. 61), but how would this progress have been possible if the society from which the state sprang, was not itself 'logically' capable of developing a state in the first place? Immaculate conceptions and mystical acts of self-creation are not even good theology these days: they can hardly be said to advance our understanding of the state.

Indeed it is worth noting that this uncritical statism represents a sharp break with the classical tradition, as Leo Strauss has shown with reference to Hegel (1945, p. 111). One of the great strengths of the classical position is its insistence that the state can be understood only if we analyse its *origins*. Unless we can say something about society before the state, we cannot understand the state itself. The origins of the state throw a critical light onto its very nature.

All the classical accounts sharply contrast the state-centred order with the world which preceded it. Plato has Glaucon speak of the 'peaceful and healthy life' of the 'original' society (1955, p. 106); the state becomes necessary as 'civilisation' is introduced. Luxuries, servants, war and a social elite all raise the temperature of the old order, and generate the kind of problems which require political philosophers to sort them out. The classical liberal tradition from Hobbes through to Rousseau sought to explain the rise of the state as a response to the 'inconveniences', 'inadequacies' or downright 'anarchy' of the state of nature, i.e. the condition that preceded the state.

Classical accounts of stateless societies differ a good deal. Plato could speak vaguely of an original *society* whereas the early liberals saddled themselves with the impossible task of trying to analyse the individual outside of society. Nevertheless what is striking is that all these accounts—even the very negative ones like the famous vignette in Hobbes—tend to stress the egalitarian and unhierarchical nature of stateless societies.

Locke introduces money in order to justify growing social divisions and the accumulation of property. Rousseau deplores the divisive role of technology and settled agriculture—'it was iron and corn which first civilised man and ruined humanity' (1973, p. 83)—while Marx and Engels emphasise the division of labour, commodity production and the institution of slavery as key factors in the rise of the state. Nozick himself, though no champion of equality, lists among other things, economies of scale, the division of labour and 'rational self-interest' as reasons why humans moved 'out of anarchy' (1974, p. 16). Whatever their other differences, all these accounts link the rise of the state with the birth of division.

Of course, much argument rages over the causalities involved. Was the burgeoning economic inequality that accompanied the rise of the state a cause or a product of political stratification, and can these elements be analytically differentiated in the pre-modern world anyway? Taylor favours the view that the formation of the state is a cause rather than a consequence of a divided community (1982, p. 133), and the pays particular attention to the way in which the fissioning of communities—their 'natural' tendency to divide and segment—is blocked by the formation of the state. Others have insisted that the state does not have one origin but many. But however we account for the emergence of the state, it is clear both from the classical tradition and those who have sought to build upon it that any critical understanding of the state *presupposes* some knowledge of its origins.

There is therefore no good reason why a focus on the state in political theory should preclude an interest in stateless societies. Uncritical statists may applaud the omission while (seemingly) critical anti-statists deplore it, but the arguments of both can be stood on their head. It is precisely because the state *is* so central to a coherent theory of politics that we must understand how it has come about. If we are really to make sense of the state, we need to know something about the mechanisms of social control which the state seeks to supplement and supplant, and how these mechanisms operate in tribal and international communities.

A concern with the origins of the state then is important in order to understand it. In particular, as we shall now see, it helps to highlight the fact that we are wrestling with an institution of a very problematic and peculiar kind. Indeed the more we broaden the historical and social context in which we analyse the state, the 'curiouser and curiouser' it actually becomes.

2 The Problem of Society

THE STATE AS A PATHOLOGICAL PARADOX

I have already argued that a state-centred concept of politics is invariably linked to a view of theory as a response to practical problems—problems of such breadth that the sovereign majesty of the state is required to sort them out. Hobbesians, who see the state as a Leviathan which brings order to a troubled world of chaos, are still obliged to acknowledge the development of the state as a product of *division*. Even uncritical statists like Crick (who are not really interested in how these divisions arise) have to note that politics exists only in societies which are 'complex and divided' (1982, p. 18). But why, it may be asked, should these divisive origins create difficulties for the state as an institution?

The problem with the state is this. It is not just a product of divisions: it is also a *producer* of divisions. It embodies and perpetuates divisions in its everyday working, for a state can be said to monopolise legitimate force only because it institutionalises a division between rulers and ruled. One of the reasons, as we shall see, why the state constitutes such a challenge to the concept of democracy is the fact that it sharply dichotomises the social order into those who have and those who have not. Hence our problem. How can it be said that the state promotes social harmony when it necessarily functions to deepen and entrench social divisions through its coercive and hierarchical machinery?

This is not just an empirical question—which states are best able to unite communities rather than divide them? It is a logical one, for how can an institution which divides people be expected at the same time to unite them? Is it to be seriously supposed that the state can create a sense of community when the very existence of its concentrated power points to the absence of the community it is supposed to create? The state is confronted by a mission impossible. It succeeds only where it is not really needed; if it is necessary, then that must mean that it is bound to fail. Hence I call the state a 'pathological paradox'. Pathological, because, as Plato reminds us, the state is called in when a once peaceful community has become feverish and troubled. Paradoxical, because if the state is to effect a cure, part of that cure must be its own redundancy.

This is why it follows that those who *do* identify the state with the principle of community and order have to project this state-engendered community and order in idealised and other-wordly terms. 'No state can find happiness', Plato tells us, 'unless the artist drawing it uses a divine pattern' (1955, p. 263). But why 'divine'? Earthly states are internally contradictory, and hence necessarily fail. If the state is to really *succeed*, then its structures have to be divinely transcendental in character. The state, in Hobbes's memorable phrase (1968, p. 227), is a 'Mortal God', and no state, according to Rousseau, has ever been founded without religion at its base (1968, p. 181). The state exudes a mystical and religious aura because it is a paradoxical institution whose very nature commits it to trying to achieve the impossible.

Rousseau elaborates this point admirably. In his discussion on the Lawgiver in *The Social Contract*, he declares: 'Gods would be needed to give men laws'. To the earthly admirer of the state who might be moved to ask why people can't make their own laws, Rousseau replies: the 'social spirit' or sense of community which the state seeks to establish would need to be present even *before* the state comes into being. For people to follow the basic rules of statecraft, the effect must become the cause (1968, pp. 84–7). Hence the role of the Gods. Only through a constant appeal to a divinely inspired justice is it possible to try and sustain the kind of communal loyalties which merely mask the divided interests of the real world.

This is why Marx (as a statist even more self critical than Rousseau) declares that the state is a 'theological concept'. It can only transcend in theory the social divisions which it embodies in practice: 'the relation of the political state to civil society is just as spiritual as the relation of heaven to earth' (1975, p. 154). Were people really to govern their own lives, they would not need an institution which concentrates and centralises power into a monopoly of legitimate force. Marx might indeed have quoted Rousseau's comment that the flaws which make states necessary 'are the same which make the abuse of them unavoidable' (1973, p. 99). Laws exist only because people *break* them. The state is therefore an institution which has to tackle problems it is congenitally incapable of solving.

Confronted then by this pathological paradox, it is not difficult to see why the anti-statists have grumbled about the unsatisfactory character of the state concept. Its problems, however, are not simply conceptual in character. They are rooted in the contradictory character of the real world, as a brief return to the clash between Dahl and Easton makes clear. Easton, we recall, identifies politics with the authoritative allocation of values for society as a whole. Dahl (1954–5, p. 483) instantly spots the 'problem'. When can it be said that an allocation is authoritative for society as a whole? Must every last man, woman and child consider it so, and where does this leave criminals and law-breakers? Dahl has a valid point. Criminals evidently do *not* believe that allocations are authoritative but if the laws against crime are not authoritative, then what are?

Dahl's predicament is this. He imagines that Easton's difficulties are purely conceptual in character—abandon a holistic definition of politics and the problem disappears! Alas, as he is later to discover, things are not so simple. In his *Modern Political Analysis* Dahl endorses, as we have already noted, Weber's definition of the state, even though a 'Government' which claims a monopoly of legitimate force has no special significance for his theory. In doing so, however, he now finds that he must meet precisely the same objections which he had himself earlier raised in relation to Easton's social-wide definition of politics.

The state, as Dahl acknowledges, seeks to monopolise force only because *rival* sources of violence challenge this monopoly with some degree of success. Criminals 'sometimes escape the law', he notes (1976, p. 12), so what kind of monopoly is this? The point, says Dahl defensively, is that the state alone has the 'legitimate' right to regulate violence, and this is a right which few would seriously contest. But here is the rub. A few, and sometimes rather more than a few, *do* contest this legitimacy as indeed they must, for the very existence of the state's legitimacy is premissed on the assumption that it is being challenged. This becomes obvious, as Dahl himself concedes, in situations of civil war where the authority of the state is openly and widely contested.

The problem, as far as Dahl is concerned, lies merely with 'the disadvantages of dichotomous definitions' (1976, p. 11). Why not put 'the Government' to one side with its divisive claim to monopolise legitimate force, and concentrate on all those little governments and political systems which felicitiously manifest the spread of power throughout society as a whole? Yet of course it is not just the definition which is 'dichotomous': it is the state itself. The state is a definitional minefield precisely because it institutionally embodies dichotomy and division: a conflict between theory and practice, between peaceful pretensions and coercive activities, between aspirations to unite and a divisive reality.

In fact, the more we probe the Weberian definition, the more vulnerable it becomes. Taylor complains that it is not enough for the state to *claim* a monopoly of legitimate force; it must actually exercise it. But this then makes the test 'far too stringent' (1972, p. 5). No matter how powerful the state is, other groups also exercise force, and at least some of these will challenge the state's 'monopoly' of legitimacy. The Mafia, the KKK, White Citizen's Councils, striking unionists and the Weathermen—Nozick's examples (to which Taylor refers)—all point to the kind of 'competitors' whose challenge to the state's monopoly of legitimate force keeps it in business. This leads Nozick himself to comment that 'formulating sufficient conditions for the existence of the state thus turns out to be a difficult and uneasy task' (1974, p. 23). Too true. But given the contradictory nature of the institution itself, has can it be otherwise?

Even theorists like Bernard Crick (who seek to confine

politics to a conciliatory world where all agree to disagree) still feel the full force of the state's paradoxical character. According to Crick, politics is conciliatory because the differing interests involved all share power in proportion to their importance to the survival of the community. But if this is so, why the need for the state?

Politics centres on the state, Crick argues, because it presupposes the existence of an institution with the acknowledged right to use force, 'if all else fails'. This is what makes it different in scale and quality from small group activity. Hence the problem. A definition of politics which chooses conciliation 'rather than violence or coercion' (1982, p. 30) slides inexorably into a definition of politics which pleads that divided societies should be ruled 'without undue violence' (1982, p. 33)—a somewhat different proposition as the hapless recipients of even a 'moderate' violence can readily testify! The paradoxical realities of the political process refuse to be soothed away by gestures of 'conciliation'.

Crick's argument reflects a contradiction which it is powerless to resolve. Each hand conflicts with the other. On the one hand, politics equals 'the public actions of free men' (1982, p. 18). But on the other hand, politics equals the right to employ sovereign force when all else fails. It is not just the 'totalitarian' Rousseau who extols the kind of freedom which forces people to be free. This is the conceptual fate of all who fall victim to the paradox of the state.

If defining the state is, in Nozick's words, a difficult and uneasy task, this is because, as I have argued above, the state itself is a difficult and uneasy institution. It exists to unify in theory only because society is divided in practice. Hence, as the consensus politics of the 1960s and 1970s begins to fade, this pathological paradox returns to the centre of political thought. Linguistic theorists may think that the state is philosophically uninteresting, and behaviouralists may grumble that it gets in the way of methodological purity. But how will criticism alone dispense with its absurdities?

Whether we disperse the concentrated power of the state into a 'ubitiquitous' definition of politics, or abolish its monopoly of legitimate force in favour of the authoritative allocation of values for society as a whole, we are still left with an institution which seeks to protect a non-existing community. For all its contradictions, the state is perfectly real! Hence its paradoxical character will take more than a few nimble formulations and definitional sleights of hand to sort out.

THE SOCIAL ROOTS OF THE POLITICAL PARADOX

We have argued so far that politics can be coherently defined only in terms of the state. If this creates difficulties, these arise not simply from the definition of the state but from its institutional (and highly problematic) reality. And the more we place the state into a social context, the more we become conscious of its contradictory nature. Understanding the state does not preclude, therefore, (as uncritical statists think) an interest in those wider social relationships which the state seeks to regulate. In fact, as we shall now argue, it presupposes it.

Indeed, just as the classical tradition demonstrates that a critical theory of the state requires some account of its origins, so it underlines also the importance of the relationship of the state to society. A critical understanding of the state requires that we focus attention on those problems within society itself which the state seek to solve. The notion expressed by latterday statists that social problems should simply be left to the sociologists, and economic problems to the economists, would have seemed absurd to classical writers. Why abstract the state from society when it is precisely here that the problems arise which the state has to try and tackle?

Hence it seems natural in *The Republic*, for example, that there is an attempt to analyse the chaos and confusion which makes the state necessary. In Plato's view, anything which erodes a time-honoured division of labour corrupts the order and virtue which needs to exist both within and between individuals in the good society. Plato's *breadth* of analysis, embracing social and economic, psychological and philsophical, biological and aesthetic dimensions flows from his concern with the state as the institution which promotes the happiness of the whole community (1955, p. 164).

Nor does this interest in the wider structures 'beyond' the state diminish with the classical liberals even if, in comparison to medieval and ancient thinkers, they now draw a much sharper analytical distinction between the state and society. It is essential to Hobbes's argument, for example, that he provide some kind of analysis of what he sees as the anti-social proclivities of an individualistic human nature. Think of the first part of the *Leviathan*, where Hobbes explores (among other things!) the nature of imagination and consciousness, language and discourse, power and the passions, and the continual drive to competition and war. The state for Hobbes is 'but an Artificial Man' whose sovereignty gives 'life and motion to the whole body' (1968, p. 81). Is there any respect of this 'whole body' or indeed, if we think of Hobbes's astonishing table of contents on the subject matter of philosophy (1968, p. 149), is there any element within the universe itself which does *not* throw light on the character of the state?

Locke's case for a 'civil government' stems from his anxiety about the 'inconveniences' of the 'state of nature'—the problems which arise when money makes it possible for individuals to accumulate property beyond their 'natural' needs. All the classical liberals, as Fine (1984, p. 12) has noted, were concerned in their different ways with what he calls the 'lack of self-sufficiency of civil society': the fact that left to its own devices, society would destroy itself through the excesses and inequalities born of private property. The state is necessary in order to try to contain deep-rooted contradictions within civil society—a difficult and challenging enterprise!

Rousseau captures this tension between state and society graphically with his dictum that 'the force of circumstance tends always to destroy equality, the force of legislation ought always tend to preserve it' (1968, p. 97). The law can be understood only in relation to the conflicts of interest it has to mediate; the General Will can be identified only through that infinity of *private* individual wills it transcends. Hence Rousseau cannot but be preoccupied with the kind of social conditions he considers necessary if the principles of political right are to stand any chance of success.

Anti-statists (as opposed to uncritical ones) do profess an interest in society at large, as we have already seen. But because they have no particular interest in the state, they necessarily ignore the social transformations which give rise to the state, and thus the contradictory character of a society which requires one. Hence the anti-statists are also uncritical as political theorists because they are uncritical about society itself. What makes classical theory critical by way of contrast, is the fact that it analyses the state in relationship to the society which it purports to 'order'. It is revealing therefore that figures whom we think of as political philsophers (like Locke) also had a deep interest in social and economic affairs, and an 'economist' like Adam Smith, for example, felt that questions of production, distribution and exchange could be understood only as part of a 'political economy'.

Indeed, as far as Smith was concerned, the 'three grand orders' which constitute society—the landowners, manufacturers and labourers—cannot merely be analysed in economic terms. Those who command the labour of others, Smith noted, have at their disposal 'the orderly oppression of the law' while those 'who labour most get least' (Fine, 1984, p. 41; Jordan, 1985, p. 56). Economics intermeshes with politics since, as Macpherson has demonstrated in detail, the classical liberals considered that it was possible to explain the state only as the product of a class-divided society. Why have a state if it is not there to defend, as Smith put it, 'those who have some property as against those who have none at all' (Macpherson, 1978, p. 108)? Social divisions make the state necessary, and yet at the same time they make it problematic. Hence the question of finding rulers who will not simply use political power to further their own particularistic interests is such a thorny one.

For Smith, independent judges are essential to maintain the 'impartiality' of public order. For Hegel, however, the problem requires a more radical solution. The contradictions inherent within the 'universal egoism' of civil society are too deeply rooted for an authentically public spirit to emerge through and beyond them. The state can arise only as a force from 'on high'. It must be imposed upon civil society from above because it cannot be derived from social interests 'below'. This is why a rational bureaucracy has a decisive role to play in Hegel's theory as the class in which a 'consciousness of right' and the 'developed intelligence' of the people is to be found (Fine, 1984, p. 63).

Of course, it is not difficult to see that Hegel's solution to this 'classical' problem is a militantly idealist one since in some kind of mysterious way, all the 'lesser wills' of society are beholden to the 'universal will' of the state. But if this is an idealist (and thoroughly mystifying) solution, it is one which is nevertheless all revealing. Given the fact that Hegel can see no 'earthly' way of tackling entrenched divisions within the social order (a conclusion which a reading of Adam Smith helped to confirm), then only an 'otherworldly' answer is possible.

The whole of the *Philosophy of Right* is premissed upon the recognition that the 'inner dialectic' of civil society increasingly promotes radical conflicts of interest which 'greatly facilitate the concentration of wealth in a few hands' (Hegel, 1967, pp. 150–1). It is because Hegel takes the basic structure and logic of a bourgeois society for granted, that no real solution to these 'natural' conflicts of interest can be found. His celebrated inversion of the state/society relationship asserts the fantastic proposition that society depends upon the state for its organisation and coherence, but this is actually Hegel's way of acknowledging (at least by implication) that in fact the opposite holds. Politics is rooted in society: society is not rooted in politics. The state has to be mystified in order to provide the *semblance* of a solution to an insoluble problem.

With Hegel, therefore, the classical tradition reaches crisis point. It is only through an apotheosis of the state—the conccept of the state as some kind of self-generating force from on high—that Hegel finds it possible to avoid an otherwise irresistible question; the question as to how an institution can transcend the social divisions which make it necessary in the first place. The 'condition', as the young Marx notes, has to be postulated as the conditioned; the determinant as the determined; the producing factor as the product of its product (1975, p. 9). The world, to put the matter plainly, has to be turned upside down and inside out. How else can Hegel evade the uncomfortable fact that the state is rooted in society as a pathological paradox—as the embodiment of impossible contradictions?

The classical tradition makes it clear that the problem of the state can be understood only within a wider context of social relationships. But this brings us face to face, however, with a fresh problem.

DISTINGUISHING THE STATE FROM SOCIETY: THE PUBLIC/PRIVATE DIVIDE

So far we have sought to defend a state-centred theory of politics by arguing that the conceptual centrality of the state is essential to a coherent view of the political process. Moreover, as we have shown, there is no reason why such a theory should be narrow. A concern with the state excludes neither an interest in the origins of the state nor in its relationship to society. In fact, for reasons we have given, it presupposes it.

But this position now saddles us with a fresh problem. If understanding the state necessitates an interest in those wider social relationships from which the state historically evolved and which it tries to regulate, are we not in fact propounding a *broad* rather than narrow concept of the state itself? If a broad view of politics jeopardises the search for a coherent definition, why should a broad view of the state by any the less troublesome? In short, we appear to have unwittingly jumped straight from the fire into the frying pan! Whether it is a broadly defined 'politics' or a broadly defined 'state' which penetrates the whole of society with its power and authority, the same problem remains. How can we locate a specific identity?

The early political theorists are notoriously unhelpful in marking the boundaries between the state and society. Ancient Greek writers like Plato and Aristotle took the view that the state is essential to the 'civilised' community, and Aristotle even defined humans as 'political animals'. The state permeates the community as a whole, and therefore the notion of a social sphere 'outside' the state is unthinkable (Sartori, 1973 p. 7). It is true, as we observed in our discussion on the origins of the state, that Plato postulates the notion of an 'original society', but since he has Glaucon rather rudely characterise this as a 'community of pigs' (1935, p. 106), it is clear that he is not tempted to analyse its implications for a coherent definition of the state.

It is really only with the rise of liberalism and its conception of an abstract, asocial individual that a sharp divorce occurs between the public and the private realm—the state and the individual—and thus by implication, between the state and society. This social realm might, liberals reflected sadly, never be able to enjoy complete and self-sufficient autonomy since the competitive drives of atomistic individuals also necessitate some correction and control by the state. Nevertheless what is significant is that with the development of liberal political thought the question of distinguishing state from society acquires a central importance.

This, it should be remembered, is no mere analytical problem: it is a moral one as well. As far as liberals are concerned, without a sharp and clear divide between the state and society, no real freedom is possible. This argument provides the overriding theme of Crick's *In Defence of Politics*, where he declares that without the existence of a private sphere outside of politics, people will find themselves at the mercy of a totalitarian state. Any attempt to politicise all social relationships, so that the line between state and society blurs, will in fact eliminate politics and with it, our liberty. 'Freedom', says Crick rather grandly, 'is the privacy of private men from public actions' (1982, p. 18). Raphael, for his part, is worried about the Greeks. The ancient view of politics as the community organised makes the state omnicompetent and so, with Raphael as with Crick, without a sharp distinction between state and society, the spectre of totalitarianism threatens (1976, p. 45).

But if it is not difficult to see why liberals should want to limit the state's powers (and thus its identity), this, it must be said, is easier said than done. Both Crick and Raphael graphically exemplify the problem. Both defend a state-centred theory of politics. The state, they rightly insist, is no ordinary social organisation. In contrast to other institutions, it is a sovereign body with a universal jurisdiction over society as a whole. It may well be that in normal times, this sovereignty lies in reserve, but there are occasions in which it has to be brought into play. With a state of emergency, for example, we become only too conscious of the fact, Crick tells us, that 'all power has to go and come from one source, if the community is to survive at all' (1982, p. 28).

But this argument poses an acute problem. On the one hand, an area of 'privacy' must be maintained as the price of freedom and yet, on the other, the state is conceived as a sovereign body, which means (to put it bluntly) that it can do what it likes. How then is the state/society distinction to be sustained? It may be that a state normally chooses not to use all its sovereign powers, but these still exist, nevertheless. After all it is the *state* itself which decides whether and how much 'autonomy' the subject is to enjoy. In a state-centred society even your right to privacy has to be protected through a framework of law. In what sense can it be said then that state and society exist apart? Sovereignty surely means what it says. The state is omnipotent: its power is 'everywhere'. An anarchist might gloomily contend that the state itself is an inherently 'totalitarian' institution incompatible with a free society, but even this position is premised on the assumption that society and the state can be separated out.

It is clear then that it is not enough simply to postulate a state/society distinction: we have to find a way of analytically sustaining it. The first question to resolve is the distinction itself. What exactly does it imply? Liberals give the impression that autonomous individuals are private because in some kind of literal and tangible sense, they are beyond the reach of the state. But in a state-centred society, individuals can live outside of the state only if at the same time they live outside of the *society* which the state regulates. Hence in the seventeenth and eighteenth centuries, liberal theory formulated the concept of a state of nature in order to entrench the absolute autonomy of individual rights. But today even radical libertarians (e.g. Rothbard, 1978a, p. 28) concede the mythical status of this classical construct, so that given the social character of the individual within a state-centred society, it is now obvious that the state/society distinction cannot be interpreted in a literalist manner.

Here Antonio Gramsci is of some help. In a celebrated passage in his *Prison Notebooks*, he argues that whereas for liberals (and he throws the syndicalists into his argument as well) the distinction between state and society is 'organic' (i.e. tangible), in fact civil and political society are 'one and the same' (1971, p. 160). The distinction between them can only be 'methodological' or analytic. We should not, in other words, expect to find any institution or Crickian individual inhabiting a niche which is literally outside or beyond the reach of the state. But how then can a purely analytical distinction be made? We turn from Gramsci to consider briefly insights into this problem drawn from Rousseau, Weber and Marx.

In the *Social Contract* Rousseau emphasises that the political will has to be 'general' in its scope so that the law can 'consider all subjects collectively and in the abstract' (1968, p. 82). A state which denied its responsibility to regulate the lives of *all* its subjects would effectively jettison its claim to sovereignty. Thus the very universality of the state's jurisdiction enables us to distinguish its laws from say the rules of a cricket club. The laws of the state bind all.

A further insight derives from Weber's notion of the state as an institution which claims a monopoly of legitimate force. This monopoly is not without its competitors—indeed, as we have seen, the state exists only because its monopoly is continually being challenged. Nevertheless the fact that the state can exercise a monopoly of force with relative if not absolute success is yet another distinct and distinguishing feature. Likewise, the force which it monopolises has to be legitimate. Unless it receives at least *some* recognition in the eyes of the public, force cannot be effectively imposed. This 'legitimacy' is of necessity a contested one but it still stands as a distinguishing feature of the state. Society as a whole may be affected by this monopoly of legitimate force but no one is under any illusion as to where its particular location lies.

The third and perhaps most crucial insight into the state's distinctive identity can be drawn from Marx's comment that the state exists as the concentrated force of society (Hoffman, 1984, p. 88). This concept of 'concentration' embraces the generalising and monopolising activities which we have already noted in Rousseau and Weber. At the same time it goes beyond them. It emphasises in particular the way in which the state gathers up the diffuse moral and social pressures which exist throughout its entire sphere of jurisdiction, and *compresses* them into the explicitly coercive instruments and formally expressed laws of a constitutional sovereign.

Nothing stands outside the state in any tangible sense. The state can derive its power from no other source than the totality of social relationships which it concentrates. On the other hand, as with the monopoly of its legitimate force and the generality of its jurisdiction, it is this activity of comprehensive concentration which sets it apart. Even if, as Mann has recently pointed out, a particular state is set up merely to institutionalise the relations between given social groups, this is done by 'concentrating resources and infrastructures in the hands of an institution that has different socio-spatial and organisational contours to those groups' (1986, p. 125). The state, in other words, has an autonomy and an identity of its own. As the 'condensation, the crystallization, the summation of social relations within its territories' (Mann, 1986, p. 132), the state is an institution whose unique attribute is that it has a hand in everything.

But how does this get us round the classical liberal dilemma of accounting for social autonomy and personal privacy within the sovereign state? How can a 'something' also be an 'everything'? If the state underpins society as a whole, in what sense can it be said to have a *distinct* identity?

We encounter not for the first, nor indeed for the last, time Hoffman's *First Law of Philosophical Obscurantism*. This states, to recall, that we can distinguish between different things only if they are same, and they can be similar only if they are also different. The notion of concentration delineated above admirably exemplifies the working of our law. The process of concentration reduces, compresses and transforms one thing into another. It links two entities together so that they cannot exist apart.

Because the state concentrates social relations, it has to draw upon society as a whole for its very existence. To that extent we can say that state and society are the 'same'. A state-centred society is an entity in its own right. All social institutions bear the mark of the state. All are affected by its underpinning role. This is why on the surface of things the broad definition of politics seems to be so plausible. Given the fact that the state concentrates society, it does indeed appear that all social phenomena are in some sense 'political'.

But it is here that the advocates of the broad definition usually lose their way. For it is precisely because the state does compress and concentrate social relationships, monopolise legitimate force, and generalise implicit norms into explicit laws that this generalising, monopolising and concentrating role makes it *distinct* from the wider society it 'condenses'. This can be only an analytical distinction because, as a 'concentrate', the state cannot be empirically separated from the relationships it concentrates. At the same time, it is a distinction of real theoretical importance because without it the unique character of the state cannot be understood.

We can therefore continue to defend the argument central to this and the previous chapter: that the concept of the state lies at the heart of a coherent definition of politics. On the other hand, what is now clear is that this definition can be a broad rather than a narrow one, and still retain the state as its conceptual focus. There is no need to follow the anti-statists by *substituting* social relationships for the state. Nor is it necessary to embrace an uncritical statism which *abstracts* the state from social relationships. We can, in other words, concede the full force of the breadth argument while avoiding the paralysing effects of an identity crisis.

Those who would push the state aside and replace it by some kind of social concept of politics, ignore the reality of its concentrated power. They are unable to inject into politics its differentiating attributes. On the other hand, those who ignore the troubled origins of the state and its contradictory relationship to society itself fail to see just how problematic the state is as an institution seeking to overcome the very social divisions which make it necessary in the first place. Both positions miss of necessity the paradoxical character of the political process.

The point about a paradox is that we can resolve it only by tackling its source, and this holds naturally enough for the state. The only way really to eliminate the kind of definitional difficulties which the state creates, is to see whether we might construct a society without one. Those who ignore the paradoxical qualities of the state, fail to pose what is perhaps one of the most exciting and challenging questions which confronts political theory in our time. Can we resolve our theoretical difficulties in politics by getting rid of the institution which practically embodies them, and in this way secure a real community in which popular self-government replaces the state?

We have already demonstrated that we can analytically distinguish state and society. Is it possible, however, to make this distinction an *empirical* one by actually dispensing with the state itself? Before we get to grips with this problem in our next chapter, some thought must be given to the following question.

WHAT WAS SOCIETY LIKE BEFORE THE STATE?

We have already argued that a critical understanding of the state necessitates some account of its origins. We must now return to this matter. If we are to tackle the question as to how we might get rid of the state, it is essential that we conclude this chapter by looking at the historical experience of those societies which have regulated their affairs without one. What mechanisms did they employ to maintain cohesion and order, and what lessons, if any, does this past experience have for the prospects of a future society which might be stateless in character?

Because the classical theorists were interested in the origin of the state, they were obliged, as we have already seen, to say something about the pre-political order. However, it has to be said that up until the nineteenth century these accounts were seriously deficient. Compounding a lack of reliable information about stateless societies was the fact that classical liberal analyses were still dominated by the concept of the state of nature. Although this celebrated construct had some positive historical consequences, which we shall evaluate in our section on democracy, it seriously obstructed an understanding of society without the state. The purpose after all of this most curious of myths was to account not simply for the rise of the state but also for its *necessity*, and this brings us face to face with the most glaring deficiency of the whole idea. By presenting the stateless world in *individual* rather than social terms, the classical liberal concept of a state of nature seemingly denied its existence as an 'order' at all.

This is most starkly obvious in Hobbes's *bellum omnium contra omnes*, and most strikingly inconsistent in Locke, where people punish one another, trade, and accumulate wealth while continuing to live in what Locke still stubbornly insists is a pre-social world. The point about the state of nature is that it cannot last. Even for Rousseau, critical as he is of social contractors who run headlong to their chains, the state is an institution which is here to stay. Hence in *The Social Contract*, where (as opposed to the *Discourses*) he is particularly concerned to legitimise the state, the 'transformation' from natural 'freedom' to social 'slavery' receives a very summary treatment—'How did this transformation come about? I do not know' (1968, p. 49)—and the portrait of people without politics is bleak. Indeed Rousseau makes it difficult to imagine how people can live in a stateless world at all, given the fact that morality and intelligence, self-mastery and freedom are qualities which, he tells us (1968, p. 65), are found only among the citizens of a legitimate state. The kind of instinctive compassion and 'self-love' which people 'naturally' possess does not allow them to form purposive or rational human relationships.

It is true that for all its abstract deficiencies, the concept of the state of nature did show *some* concern for the problem of the pre-political order. Utilitarians, who later poked fun at the classical notion of natural rights, for example, as 'nonsense on stilts', lost all interest in the question of what society was like before the state. In general, it can be said that those who are happy to accept the 'idealism of the state' at face value, show little inclination to pursue the question any further. At best, life without the state is a purely negative condition—an 'anarchy' to avoid (Southall, 1968, p. 167). After all, the very credibility of politics is at stake. If it can be shown that people have at some point in the past lived without politics, this can only puncture (at least some of) the pretentious majesty of the sovereign state. You wish to find a way of getting rid of the state or at least cutting it down to size? Then the first thing you must establish is that this is an institution which has not always been around.

It is true that the anti-statists we looked at earlier are critical of the *concept* of the state, and express an interest in stateless societies. But the significance of these historical 'anarchies' is lost if they are merely treated as the examplars of a 'ubiquitous' politics, and no attempt is made to contrast the regulatory mechanisms of a state-centred society with those which exist in a society without one.

Of course, anti-statists may actually tell us rather more about the character of stateless societies than their theory would appear to allow. Leftwich in his *Redefining Politics* provides a graphic picture of the !Kung San people of the Kalahari. He notes the fact (echoing Engels's famous comment about the Iroquois) that they have no police, standing armies or law-enforcement agencies. Leadership is informal and inconspicuous, and the power to make decisions vests in the ordinary members of the community, who actively participate in running their own lives (1983, p. 37).

Compare this system or the co-operative institutions of the pastoral Masai of East Africa with the 'predatory politics' of the Aztecs of Central America, and the contrast is dramatic. Here, Leftwich tells us, power was highly concentrated in the hands of a patriarchal ruler who enjoyed an almost godlike supremacy over his people, and who was buttressed by a powerful ruling class composed of civil, military and religious elites. Slavery, absent among the !Kung San or the Masai, was now crucial to the economy, and the continuous drive to war acted as a central mechanism for exacting tribute from neighbouring regions.

However, none of this unfortunately helps Leftwich in his attempt to 'redefine' politics, for what is the point of labelling two antithetical modes of organisation as both 'political' when what needs to be explained is the fact that the way in which each governs their respective society is so strikingly different? Anti-statists, who analyse stateless societies concretely, merely highlight the untenably *abstract* character of their own definitions. In the same way, anthropologists may provide invaluable information about pre-literate societies without necessarily placing any particular emphasis on the contrast between stateless and state-centred orders.

Yet what is clear even from accounts like these is that in many respects stateless societies were far *more* orderly than the state-centred societies which succeeded them. They were also more participatory and caring. Sceptics might even wonder which type of society is the more 'civilised'. As genuine communities of people with real interests in common, these stateless orders required no 'illusory community' imposed from on high to keep them from falling apart. Indeed, what they graphically demonstrate is that the Hobbesian war of all against all, as Rousseau had already begun to suspect (1973, p. 65–6), is not humanly natural but historically social—the product of a society in which irreconcilable conflicts of interest at once necessitate, and are at the same time perpetuated by the concentrated powers of the state. A stateless society raises precisely the question which the Hobbesian argument tries to suppress: namely how do people govern their lives, order their existence, and relate peaceably to one another in the absence of the state?

We do not need to suppose that in a stateless society, there are no conflicts at all. Indeed Roberts (1979) is just one of many anthropologists who have analysed in detail the way in which disputes in stateless societies are settled. We may safely presume that quarrels, disputes, disagreements, even 'crimes of passion' are endemic in all social relationships, state-centred or otherwise. But the crucial point about a stateless society is that no monopoly of legitimate force exists (or is required) to sort problems like these out.

Indeed stateless societies are not always societies without *war*. Armed clashes between rival clans over, say, disputed hunting grounds may occur but as with less serious quarrels, the point about them is that they are not prosecuted in a statist manner. Wars are not fought by standing armies; they are waged by volunteers. Defeated enemies are not enslaved or imprisoned—they are either integrated into the victorious clan or banished from the territory. Wars arise when the established rhythms of hunting or food gathering are disturbed: they do not function as the driving force of a predatory economy. Feuds may well be ferocious and bloody but, as Engels emphasises (1972, p. 159), they relate to the settlement of disputes by the community itself.

Roberts (1979, pp. 117–19) provides a fascinating account of how the Jale people of New Guinea resolve their differences through fighting rather than by means of discussion, although it should be noted that this fighting is highly formalised and carefully contained so as to minimise disruption to the life of the community. War and warlike activities do not involve specialised agencies standing outside ordinary society, and invoking concentrated powers which are imposed 'from above'.

Clearly then stateless societies are societies which have to be governed and regulated. (For a now classic account, see Mair, 1962.) This 'government' involves coercion, to be sure, but it does not necessitate the state. The practice of sharing food and exchanging gifts, for example, generates a widespread sense of 'reciprocity', which can be reduced or withdrawn as a mark of disapproval. The fear of incurring violent retaliation; ostracism and excommunication; expulsion from the community; shaming or public ridicule; the threat of sorcery and the invocation of supernatural sanctions—all these, as Taylor has shown in detail (1982, pp. 65–90), involve what J.S. Mill called a social 'despotism' or moral coercion (1974, p. 68). They do not (or need not), however, involve the state. There may even be some inequality and role differentiation along sex and age lines in stateless societies but the concentration of power which flows from this is still limited, and does not allow for any institution with a monopoly of legitimate force.

It is therefore unnecessary to present these early stateless societies in any kind of idealised or 'utopian' way. Indeed, modern liberals may well protest that far from being chaotic and conflict-ridden, these 'anarchies' were *too* orderly. They were societies in which individuality itself was threatened by the cohesive collectivism of tribe and clan. There may be some truth in this criticism. What it suggests, however, is not that these 'anarchic' societies lacked government but that on the contrary, they were governed too well! Certainly they constitute an important conceptual resource for those challenging the eternal need for a state, and seeking to project a future without one.

Nevertheless it might be objected that these stateless societies (many of which no longer exist today in their original form) do no more than demonstrate the *logical* possibility of governing society without the state. They may even help to highlight the paradoxical character of the state as an 'illusory community'. But in practical terms they offer no real guidance as to how one might set about establishing a stateless society in the future.

This is the problem to which we now wish to turn.

3 Getting Rid of the State

WHAT HOPE FOR THE FUTURE?

Logically, the experience of the historical 'anarchies' suggests that stateless societies are possible. But how likely are they in today's world? How could they be brought about? These were (and in some cases still are) societies which existed before the state: what do they tell us about the prospects of society *after* the state? Indeed it could well be argued that these 'early' societies demonstrate just how difficult in fact it would be to get rid of the state, since the conditions which have made state-lessness possible in the past could not conceivably be replicated in the future.

Two problems in particular deserve our attention here. The first and most telling is that in these 'early' societies, the absence of a state is a product of economic backwardness. These are societies rooted in clan and tribal structures sustained by an extremely rudimentary mode of production: they are incapable of generating significant amounts of wealth, and thus of maintaining a large population.

This is why Marxist accounts, for example, usually (if not wholly felicitously) refer to the 'primitive' communism of these societies, with their constitutions of 'childlike simplicity' based on the 'immature' development of a people yet to sever their 'umbilical cords' (e.g. Engels, 1972, pp. 159–61). The society of the future must arise (Engels quotes the words of Lewis Morgan) as the revival 'in a *higher* form' of the liberty, equality and fraternity of the ancient clans (1972, p. 237, our italics). Past (or even present) examples of stateless societies cannot, in other words, simply be taken as models for the future. Marxists place a special emphasis upon the need for *abundance*, and capitalism receives ironic praise for its 'constant revolutionising' of production—for providing the basis for a classless and stateless society of the future.

This question of backwardness helps to focus upon a second difficulty in trying to get rid of the state: the problem of scale and intimacy. The kind of non-statist social controls which substituted for the state in the past have all operated in small-scale societies, where reciprocal relationships can be sustained by frequent, physical contact of an all-round kind. How would this level of intimacy be possible in the complex, populous and industrialised societies necessary to underpin the self-governing communities of the future?

The world we live in is one in which a sense of global interdependence is becoming more obvious every day. Increasingly, our communities have not only transcended tribal and clan loyalties, but are expanding beyond national boundaries as well. Ours is a world based on growing co-ordination and planning (even when this occurs within the competitive cut and thrust of a capitalist economy), and on a permanent revolution in science and technology. The old forms of social control—shaming and public ridicule, the invocation of supernatural sanctions and sorcery—are not only archaic, but the resort to fissioning and feuding, secession and occasional war now appear to be grotesquely inappropriate (not to say potentially self-destructive) ways of settling disputes.

Would it be possible to replace them with other forms of social control which would be more relevant, and yet still retain their non-statist character? Is there any prospect that the technological revolution in communications might help to generate among millions of people that sense of community and intimacy which in the past was only feasible among small-scale societies with a sparse population? One thing certainly is clear: the tribal societies of the past cannot stand as models for the stateless society of the future.

But what of the other example of stateless order which is so often cited—the supra-political institutions of the international community? Are these not 'anarchic' forms of regulation which demonstrate the possibility of living 'beyond' the state? The problem here is that diplomacy and peace treaties, international conferences and accords are all entered into by existing *states*. It is hard to see these activities as organisational alternatives to sovereign acts of statehood since, in the context of the international community, it is precisely sovereign states who constitute the 'stateless' actors. Furthermore, their numbers are increasing rather than diminishing. Both externally as well as internally, the state appears to be playing a greater rather than a lesser role in the life of communities: not, it might be thought, a particularly propitious environment in which to consider the prospects for getting rid of the state!

Moreover, the states system of the international world poses yet another problem: how could one state be expected to dissolve its concentrated powers unless all other states immediately followed suit? The problem of how we could even *begin* to move towards a world without the state appears formidable indeed.

It is difficult to get round the assertion that however interesting stateless societies, past or present, tribal or international, are or might have been, they offer no real help for the future. In fact, it might even be argued that they actually reinforce the very point which those who diligently study them often wish to rebut—namely the practical impossibility of getting rid of the state in an advanced industrial world. At best, the evidence of the past is inconclusive. At worst, it provides yet another obstacle in the path of those who seek to resolve the definitional difficulties of the state by eliminating the very institution which constitutes the source of their problems.

Nevertheless not all political theorists feel completely helpless in the face of such a challenge. We turn to examine the first of two rival strategies (and the variants within them) for dispensing with the services of the state.

REFURBISHING THE STATE OF NATURE: THE LIBERTARIAN SOLUTION

We have already noted that many political theorists either reject the state as an important concept in political theory, or they follow the traditional view that the state is so essential to an orderly and civilised life that it would neither be possible nor desirable to live without one. But what of those who do think that speculation about a world without the state is a worthwhile and potentially rewarding activity?

They basically divide into two camps. One favours an individualistic, the other a communitarian solution to the problem of the state. Consider first the individualistic solution: the arguments of those who, camped on the wilder shores of the New Right, call for what they are pleased to describe as 'libertarian' solutions.

Libertarians believe that it is possible to have a society (or at least 'an aggregate of individuals') in which the right to own property and enjoy traditional civil liberties can be exercised either without the state at all, or at least with a state whose powers have been drastically curtailed. Libertarians therefore subscribe enthusiastically to Bastiat's iconoclastic view of the state as 'the great fictitious entity by which everyone seeks to live at the expense of everyone else' (Barry, 1981, p. 60). As this quotation suggests, what they object to most about the state is that it erodes the independence of the private-property-owning individual.

Not surprisingly, libertarians feel attracted to Locke rather than Marx, and believe that the Lockean state of nature with its timeless natural laws based upon the inalienable rights of the abstract individual, still has relevance to the modern world. While they are wary of the coercive powers of the state, they are not impressed by the argument that the state may also play a caring welfare role, since it is precisely in the expansion of a public service sector that libertarians find the greatest threat to individual freedom. Here, they argue, property rights are continuously eroded in the name of the public interest, and the incentive to hard work is undermined by high taxation. Besides, they insist, spending on welfare is no less coercive than infringing civil rights because the point about taxes is that they *have* to be paid. Expanding the service sector of the state is merely an underhand way of radically enhancing its monopoly of legitimate force.

All libertarians agree that it is quite improper for the state to oblige citizens to help one another, or to prevent activities which do not directly harm others. All strongly oppose a 'positive' or welfare role for the state. However, some (with Nozick as perhaps the most celebrated modern example) shrink from anarchism proper, and argue merely for a 'minimal' state in which political coercion is strictly confined to the task of protecting property and enforcing contracts. But this 'half-way house' solution runs into a number of logical and practical snags (as more radical libertarians waste no time in pointing out), for once you actually have a state, how do you prevent it from continually expanding its scope and powers?

Assume a state with a narrowly defined 'law and order' role. It is not to regulate the economy or provide welfare services to its citizens. Yet such state cannot fulfil even this limited role effectively in the modern world unless certain conditions obtain. It must, for example, have healthy recruits for its armed services, a reasonably literate police force, and a reliable source of supply of arms and ammunition. Where the 'private sector' fails to deliver on any of these fronts (think of the problem of malnourished recruits for the Boer War in Britain at the turn of the century), state intervention is necessary simply in order to ensure that the state is really able to fulfil its 'limited' role. This is why whenever the state goes to war, for example, (an activity which minimal statists must surely allow) we invariably witness the drastic extension of its 'positive' activities if only to guarantee its 'negative' functions.

The same difficulty arises out of the state's monopoly of legitimate coercion. This irksome infringement of the principle of free competition is justified by minimal statists like Nozick on the grounds that the provision of protection by rival agencies is too 'risky' for society. The state is entitled to its monopoly because it compensates potential competitors by providing its protection free i.e. through a general charge on the public purse. But it is not difficult to see that this is a principle capable of an almost infinite extension.

After all, the expansion of the state into a wide range of social activities—from the provision of low-cost housing to the nationalisation of essential but unprofitable industries—can be justified on precisely these grounds. These are also activities, it might be argued, which are too 'risky' and 'unproductive' for private entrepreneurs to invest in, and the involvement of the state, though monopolist in character, can be compensated for by providing free or subsidised services for those excluded. One you have a state, how do you stop it expanding?

Consider the classical liberal argument that the state must merely protect rather than support individuals in society. Where do you draw the line? The New Liberals of the late nineteenth century showed just how painlessly the notion of 'protection' can be broadened. Can people really feel 'secure' if they have no job? Are contracts respected if the rich take advantage of the poor? Must not the state intervene when people are robbed of their land by speculators, or of their labour power though exploitation? If the state has the role of *protecting* individuals, then virtually every activity it undertakes can find justification. In short, it seems impossible for a minimal state to be cabined, cribbed and confined in the way Nozick proposes.

As far as the full-blooded libertarian is concerned, it is necessary therefore to dispense with the state altogether. Protection should be provided *privately*. People could insure themselves against bodily assault, for example, just as they currently insure their possessions against theft. Aggrieved parties would secure compensation for injury via 'informal' courts and tribunals. Even in statist societies, maximalist libertarians argue, an increasing number of citizens are already turning to private arbitrators to settle their insurance claims. These arbitrations rely upon mutual agreement rather than courts of law to enforce them, and in a stateless world able to accurately disseminate data about a person's willingness to comply with commitments freely entered, ostracism and boycotts could be potent sanctions against defaulters. Moreover, insurance companies could always hire private police to tackle those who refuse to fall into line (Rothbard, 1978b, p. 201).

This argument certainly avoids the problems faced by the minimal state, but at what cost! After all, it should not be forgotten that the whole point about Locke's state of nature is that at the end of the day rational individuals feel obliged to leave it. It is true that the 'inconveniences' suffered seem somewhat trivial in comparison with the turbulent chaos of a

Hobbesian war of all against all, but they are real nevertheless. What is more to the point, they are an intrinsic part of the 'natural' order. Without a state to surmount them, Lockean 'inconveniences' become a source of paralysis and collapse.

Two problems in particular confront libertarians in their search for an alternative to the state. The first is the nature of the market. In libertarian eyes, the market always decentralises and disperses power; it is the only the state which concentrates it. Yet it is significant that in Locke's (and Nozick's) state of nature, the spontaneous activity of individuals generates inequality, and Nozick himself accepts that as individuals compete to provide themselves with protection, a dominant protection agency (the forerunner of the minimal state) will necessarily emerge. The tendency for competition to create informal concentrations of power is widely accepted by all but the most doctrinaire economists. Left to its own devices, the market inevitably strengthens the strong and weakens the weak. To present the market as an *alternative* to the state ignores the fact therefore (which the classical liberals readily acknowledged) that the very need for a state arises out of the divisive consequences of the market itself.

Libertarians can sustain their unreal view of the market only by abstracting individuals from all those social relationships through which they exercise differential amounts of power. The libertarian scenario with its arbitrators and private law-suits assumes a world, as one critic puts it, of 'shared interests and common peers' (Stone, 1978, p. 210). But what of a situation in which, say, a large corporation pollutes the environment or sells defective products, thereby inflicting injury upon a large number of relatively defenseless and un-organised individuals? This is the activity of a private 'individual' only in the sense that it is the activity of a private individual *institution* relatively state-like in its monopolistic exercise of power. The notion that the world is composed of discrete individuals all roughly equal in the amount of clout they wield is an illusion, and it creates the second major problem for libertarian opponents of the state. This is the problem of what are often called 'externalities' or 'spillovers'.

Externalities or spillovers arise as the unintended social consequences of individual acts, and they create problems for the libertarian case whether they take a positive or a negative form. Negative externalities (like a factory polluting the environment) are a problem because the costs of such an activity are much less to the offending agent than they are to society at large. It is not therefore in anyone's *individual* interest to pay the extra needed to eliminate the problem. Unless the problem is tackled collectively (with appropriate pressures being brought to bear on offending individuals), it won't be tackled at all.

Positive spillovers or externalities also create difficulties. They arise in a situation in which people benefit from a particular activity without having to pay for it, i.e. where the property of 'non-excludability' has beneficial rather than deleterious consequences for society in general. A simple example. Householders build a wall around their property: how are they to prevent neighbours from having protection provided free of charge?

This kind of 'problem', to take a slightly more complicated example, could have fatal consequences for the commercial viability of, say, a private protective agency in a situation where some but not all the householders in a neighbourhood take out premiums for policing services. The presence of police in the neighbourhood provides a 'spillover' non-excludable deterrent effect: all benefit from the actions of some. Not surprisingly, the premium payers, having an acute sense of their own self-interest as 'rational' libertarians, fail to see why they should provide charity for their neighbours. They cease their contributions forthwith, and the service collapses sabotaged by the spontaneous generation of positive spillovers. There is of course a solution to this kind of problem but it is one which is all revealing.

Why not insist, as a way of tackling this particular difficulty, that *all* have to insure their properties before any one individual becomes committed? A sensible enough proposition, but one which explodes the very foundation of the libertarian argument! For if people have to co-operate socially in order to protect their interests as individuals, then individualism itself (as an abstract creed) is turned inside out. The 'society', which is supposed not to exist, manifests its all too tangible collectivity as a whole clearly greater than the sum of its parts. Isn't this precisely the (sinister and 'totalitarian') point which Rousseau makes in *The Social Contract* when he says that everyone must give up everything to the communty if a true association of individuals is to be secured (1968, p. 60)?

In other words, as critics have been quick to emphasise, a stateless society could operate along libertarian lines only when everyone was roughly equal as the members of a common community. But this is surely an odd stipulation for a philosophy which sets itself against all forms of egalitarianism, and which sees in individual self-aggrandisement, the essence of real freedom.

A purely market rationality based upon individual self-interest turns out to be collectively self-defeating.

MARXIST AND ANARCHIST STRATEGIES: A PRACTICAL ANSWER?

Libertarians, as we have seen, are opposed to the state because it infringes individual rights and the unimpeded exercise of private property. Communitarians take a much more social view of the problem. The state, they argue, is objectionable because it both reflects and reinforces deep-rooted conflicts of interest, and thus stands as a barrier to the very existence of a real community. Property, they argue, embodies social power, and hence should be subject to social regulation. If it continues to be privately owned, this has to be justified in the light of community interests and communal principles.

This stance, however, confronts communitarians with the following dilemma. Whereas libertarians profess to accept 'human nature' as it is, i.e. people as producers and consumers, employers and employees in a capitalist society, communitarians seek to restructure the world. Genuine communities will become possible only if human nature itself is changed. But how? Unless people can change this human nature *themselves*, will we not merely witness the exchange of one set of masters for another?

The problem, as always, is acutely presented by Rousseau—so much so that we are tempted to call it 'Rousseau's paradox'. For the paradox is this. People are called upon to govern themselves when they are 'everywhere in chains'. Yet if people are enslaved, how can they become free without the special assistance of some kind of force from 'on high'? It is over Rousseau's paradox that communitarians divide. Just as some libertarians accept the need for a minimal state, so some communitarians argue the case, not for a minimal state, but for a *transitional* one—for what might be called a politics to end all politics.

This, in a nutshell, is what differentiates anarchists on the one hand from Marxists on the other. As far as anarchists are concerned, it makes no sense to oppose one concentration of power by another, and therefore the Marxist argument that exploited workers need to organise politically is absurdly self-defeating. Oppressive hierarchies are oppressive hierarchies, whether this is the hierarchy of the state under capitalism, the revolutionary party which challenges it, or the dictatorship of the proletariat. As at least one celebrated anarchist turned authoritarian has put it, whoever says organisation says oligarchy. The Marxist strategy is a recipe for certain betrayal.

There can be no doubt that Rousseau's paradox poses real problems for those seeking to get rid of the state. How then do the anarchists propose to tackle the problem of governing yourself when you are everywhere in chains? Here their case begins to falter. Anarchists generally speak about the virtues of 'spontaneity' as a mode of protest which eschews the oligarchic dangers of organisation. The popular masses, they argue, are either seething with indignation against the iniquities of statist oppression, or would be if only they were conscious of their real interests.

It is, however, hard to see how this argument can avoid falling foul of Rousseau's paradox. If, on the one hand, the people are as the anarchists say seething with discontent and wish to overthrow their oppressors, why don't they simply get on with the job? If on the other hand, the time is not ripe, and they must wait wait for guidance, leadership, enlightenment or inspiration before liberating themselves, the more suspiciously like *organised* activity their 'spontaneous' 'self-activity' appears to become. Any suggestion that the people are not automatically conscious of their 'real' interests points to that very gulf between leaders and led which the anarchists are supposed to spontaneously transcend.

But perhaps an anarchist strategy to tackle Rousseau's paradox (and thus get rid of the state) might adopt a more modest tack. Instead of sweeping away the edifice of the state (and all other oppressive hierarchies) through a spontaneous uprising, why not establish in one's own locality an 'island' of anarchism? This is not so much a question of eagerly studying the behaviour of people in queues or drivers who all stay on the same side of the road (as in Laver's entertaining analysis of the 'anarchy of everyday life', 1983, p. 52) as it is of consciously propagating alternatives. Setting up a commune; establishing a co-operative; cultivating a different life-style; forging a counter-culture. Propagating alternatives like these will, it is hoped, gradually undermine the state from within as more and more people simply 'opt' out of a statist way of life, and rely upon social rather than political controls to regulate their existence.

Yet if this 'incrementalist' version of anarchist strategy appears rather more plausible than the belief in spontaneous insurrection, it still suffers from serious problems. Take the question of co-operatives, for example. In a capitalist society economic units which do not make a profit do not survive; and a co-operative which is to prosper has to buy and sell its goods in the wider market. It is confronted with the problem of competing with capitalists who use managerial hierarchies to cut costs, and who rely upon the state to maintain labour 'discipline' and provide lucrative contracts. Does this not present co-operatives with the unpalatable choice of either imitating their 'hierarchical' competitors or going bankrupt?

This problem of operating in a 'hostile' environment raises a further difficulty, and one which faces both the insurrectionary and 'incremental' anarchist alike. Given the political realities of an institution which monopolises legitimate force, why should we suppose that the state will passively yield to a radical challenge from anarchistic adversaries intent on promoting its demise? A 'spontaneous' uprising, even when it does eventually materialise, is unlikely to succeed if it is met by the armed might of a well-organised state. Co-operatives, alternative life-styles and other islands of anarchism are no match for the authoritarian sweep of a Leviathan on the attack.

It is to deal with objections like these that Marxists have

always argued that the struggle for a stateless and classless society has to be *political* in character. Workers and their popular allies need to organise themselves into trade unions, movements and parties in order to win the 'battle of democracy', using their 'political supremacy' to 'centralise all instruments of production in the hands of the State' (Marx and Engels, 1976b, p. 504).

Military analogies abound in Marxist writings. Party members are likened by Gramsci, for example, to disciplined soldiers; party leaders to 'Generals' who need to organise their rank and file (1971, p. 152). The centralised might of capital must be met with the centralised might of the workers if the class *war* is to be successfully prosecuted. A revolution, Friedrich Engels once declared, is the 'most authoritarian thing there is' (Hoffman, 1984, p. 168). Without the concentrated power of the 'people', how is to possible to dislodge the concentrated power of capital and its state? Not only must workers politically organise to oust their enemies but they must establish their own state if the new socialist order is to survive. The fate of the Paris Commune or Allende's Chile offers painful testimony to this point.

All this would appear to demonstrate Rousseau's paradox with a vengeance. As we have already seen, it is an argument which makes the anarchists extremely uneasy. If revolutionaries take part in politics, will we not simply see one elite replacing another? Why should the 'dictatorship of the proletariat' be any the less oppressive than the dictatorship of the bourgeoisie? It may seem realistic to organise politically in order to get rid of politics but is it not self-defeating?

The actual historical experience of Marxist theory in practice bears these objections out, say the anarchists, with the 'fate' of the Russian Revolution being a case in point. Even before Joseph Stalin had become General Secretary of the Communist party, power had become tightly centralised under Lenin, the opposition dissolved, and political liberties curtailed. Moreoever, continues the argument, Stalin's own personality cult and his 'theological' inquisitions bear out in gruesome form Rousseau's observation that religion forms the basis of every state.

These angry reflections have not, of course, been confined to the anarchists. Both New Left and New Right theorists have also expressed their profound scepticism about the prospects of existing Marxist states ever 'withering away'. In practice, they argue, the Marxist theory of using politics to end politics has simply served to inflate dramatically the power of the state. (See, e.g. the comments of Barry, 1981, p. 56 and Hall, 1984b, p. 24.) What then do Marxists, particularly those of an 'Old Left' (or classical) orientation, have to say in their defence?

Basically they argue that revolutionary 'proletarian' politics is qualitatively different from the conservative politics of the old order. It is emphatically not, as the anarchists contend, a question of simply engaging in oppressively hierarchical modes of organisations, and then hoping that, at the some indeterminate point in the future, the state will magically wither away. Its *transitional* character is inherent in Marxist politics from the start. The mass involvement of people in politics involves a logic of 'democratic centralism'—that is to say, a process in which decentralisation is, in Lenin's words, 'an essential prerequisite to revolutionary centralisation and an essential corrective to it' (Hoffman, 1984, p. 73). Marxist politics is a politics of participation: a politics which increasingly erodes the old division between society and the state. Organisation and planning now serve to concentrate power and wealth in the hands of the people so that gradually, the state's monopoly of legitimate force is dissolved back into institutions of a purely social character.

Marxists naturally plead numerous practical difficulties in realising this scenario in the contemporary world. Socialist societies, they point out, are being constructed in countries which were formerly backward and undeveloped. These societies are compelled by their unsympathetic capitalist rivals to devote significant amounts of their resources to nuclear arsenals and sophisticated weaponry—a most statist activity if ever there was one. As newly established orders (relatively speaking), they are reluctant to dismantle speedily their state apparatuses lest this enables domestic and foreign adversaries to undermine their social structures. This of course also reflects the problem noted earlier of one state or indeed even one group of states dissolving away their concentrated power while other states remain very much intact.

Nevertheless Soviet party leaders insist for example that in the USSR statehood is being gradually tranformed into 'communist self-government'. But this process of transition must be seen as one which is moving forward (understandably perhaps) at a rather modest pace—although the new leadership with Mikhail Gorbachev at the helm does seem to taking a much more dynamic view of this problem.

However, the anarchists and other critics of 'existing socialism' are not usually impressed, for the difficulty which the Marxists (or the 'official Marxists' as they are sometimes called) have is this. Under socialism as it currently exists, millions of people participate in political activity. They take part in organising elections, in factory, farm and neighbour-hood committees, in demonstrations and discussions, in planning and policing—in activities many of which remain the prerogative of a small elite in liberal capitalist societies.

But at the same time no Marxist can really deny that these mass activities 'from below' are also led and controlled 'from above'. They take place with the support of the socialist state, and under the 'guidance' of party leaderships. For this reason, say the anarchists, none of this mass participation really 'counts'. Why can't people organise themselves *against* the state, and in ways of which the party leaders *don't* approve? The Gorbachev era is beginning to reveal a new self-confidence on the part of the socialist state, but thus far 'grass roots opposition' has yet to become an established political tradition within existing socialist societies.

Hence the scepticism which Marxists invariably encounter. The notion of a politics to end all politics invites us to accept that people with power will increasingly hand it back to society simply because they are leaders and functionaries of a 'new type'. Is it realistic, ask the critics, to suppose that those with concentrated power will yield it up unless they are subject at the same time to real pressures 'from below': pressures which are sufficiently sustained and compelling to remind socialist politicians of the 'transitional' character of the socialist state?

This point is worth taking seriously. Whatever one thinks of the Marxist argument (and not everyone finds its logic compelling), there can be little doubt that until there is more striking evidence of popular autonomy and critical independence among the mass organisations of a socialist society, there will continue to be this scepticism about the 'transitional' state as an historical reality. Those accustomed to the 'private' institutions of a liberal society will want to see tighter controls *over* the transitional state under socialism before they find the Marxist case convincing. If the state *is* slowly dissolving itself back into society in the existing socialist world, there are not many political theorists outside the Old Left Marxist camp who view things that way. (For a recent assessment of this problem, see Dawisha, 1986.) There may be a logical case for the transitional state but, ask the sceptics, is there an empirical one? All the evidence, as Levine (1987, p. 172) puts it, is 'by no means in', and this means inevitably that the bearing of 'the pertinent available data' is disputable.

We have to conclude therefore that arguments about getting rid of the state remain highly controversial. The Marxists find it difficult to persuade their critics that this process is already under way while the anarchists for their part tend to retreat into utopia or despair. A recent work on democracy, however, suggests optimistically that a multiplicity of authorities with specialised competences could be co-ordinated in society 'without being subordinate to any single overarching authority'. But here is the rub. Such a state of affairs would presuppose that society did not, as the author puts it, 'generate organisations with interests that were so wide ranging, self-contained and strong as to enable them to defy community sanctions' (Burnheim, 1985, p. 21).

A realistic assumption? We live in a world in which power is *already* concentrated in organisations strong enough to defy community sanctions. The chains are all around us: hence our desire for freedom. It is precisely because these organisations do exist that states with their monopoly of legitimate force have developed in the first place. Take away powerful property owners and privileged corporations, multi-national capitalists and international financiers, and arguably we have moved at least some of the way towards making the state redundant. But how is this to be done?

This is the question which the 'painless optimists' fail to address. Rousseau's paradox remains insoluble unless we come to terms with the unpalatable truth that it takes one

Leviathan to get rid of another. As Levine (1987, p. 18) puts it crisply, states are indispensable to statelessness. Unless we can find some kind of way of turning politics against itself, no progress seems possible. It is this predicament which sobers up the Marxists and makes the anarchists so gloomy.

Getting rid of the state is a problematic business—but it does at least have one positive consequence for the argument we have been developing. It compels us to focus as sharply as we can on the state as a distinct and separable entity: after all, the best way of showing that society and the state can be differentiated is to construct a society without one. In that way, an analytical differentiation can become quite tangible! This, I have argued, is certainly a logical possibility, and it may even be an empirical one.

Nevertheless this is not the end of the matter. For the elusive paradoxes of the state haunt political theory as a whole. This will become readily apparent as we turn to consider the second of the contentious concepts of our contestable triad, the problem of power.

PART TWO
POWER AND AUTHORITY

4 Machiavelli's Centaur and the Two Levels

THE CONTRADICTORY RELATIONSHIP

We have attempted in the previous section to differentiate the state from society in a way which enables us to identify politics coherently. But this still leaves us the problem of trying to make sense of an institution which monopolises 'legitimate violence'. This celebrated formula is, when we think about it, a highly perplexing one, for how can it be said that force is ever 'legitimate'?

This is the conundrum we want to explore in the next three chapters. In essence, the problem can be expressed as follows. Violence or naked power appears inherently illegitimate and immoral in character, and yet in Weber's definition, we encounter both legitimacy *and* force brought together in the institution of the state.

We have, in other words, a further dimension to add to the paradox explored in the previous section. The state, as we have seen, seeks to secure the common good through dividing the community. Now we must confront the fact that the state can act in this contradictory way only because the violence it invokes is 'legitimate'. It seems contrary to common sense and logical precept that an institution should be able to project its moral injunctions through acts of brute force. Yet this is what states do all the time: how is it possible?

Political theory has traditionally grasped the fact that no state can sustain itself through brute force alone. Even gangsters or thieves need a 'unity of purpose' if they are to succeed, as Plato points out (1955, p. 83), and no theorist, past or present, has ever claimed that the state can function unless it is able to secure at least *some* support for its actions. It is revealing, for example, that although Hobbes dramatically emphasises the need for a Leviathan to employ 'terror' (1968, p. 227), he also stresses that this terror must arise through 'consent'. The 'Mortal God' must be 'authorised' by the people whose lives it orders. The state is the product of a social contract—a mutual agreement between rulers and ruled.Even elitists hostile to classical liberalism like Vilfredo Pareto have argued that the governing classes maintain themselves in power 'partly by force and partly by the consent of the governed' (Cox, Furlong and Page, 1985, p. 82).

This is a problem which particularly interested Antonio Gramsci. He called it the problem of the 'two levels': legitimacy on the one hand, and force on the other. Gramsci traces this dual perspective back to Machiavelli's centaur, the mythical half-animal half-human creature which his great Renaissance ancestor had seen as an allegory or metaphor for politics in general. Machiavelli speaks of two ways in which humans fight—through law and by force—and in his *Prison Notebooks*, Gramsci uses different terms to describe the two moments of the Machiavellian centaur: coercion and consent, violence and civilisation, political and civil society, state and church, authority and hegemony (1971, p. 170). But however we characterise them, Gramsci's antinomies are central to the problem I want to focus upon here, the problem of power and authority.

Like Gramsci, theorists today often employ a variety of terms in analysing the same conceptual problem. For the sake of consistency, I shall assume that the concept of 'power' corresponds broadly with the idea of coercion or force, and the concept of authority with the notion of morality or consent. But whatever their terminology, all political theorists are conscious nevertheless of the need to distinguish between power and authority. The question is—how?

Norman Barry concedes that it is quite unsatisfactory to argue, as a simple-minded moralist might, that power pertains to things as they actually *are* in political life, while the question of authority relates to things as they *ought to be* (1981, p. 68). After all unless the practical exercise of power on a daily basis can acquire some legitimacy, the political order itself will crumble. Both power and authority are part of real politics but how is the linkage between them sustained?

This problem particularly bothers Rousseau. Might, Rousseau insists, can never be transformed into right, for 'force is a physical power; I do not see how its effects could produce morality' (1968, p. 52). Yet Rousseau is equally adamant: people must obey the law. It is no good enjoying the rights of a citizen unless you also undertake the duties of a subject. The social contract would be a worthless formula were it not for the fact that whoever refuses to obey the general will shall be 'constrained to do so'. People must, in that most celebrated of phrases, be 'forced to be free' (1968, p. 64). But how is this possible? If force negates morality, how can it constitute an essential component of the General Will? Even if we accept Rousseau's ingenious proposition that you merely obey laws which you prescribe to yourself, can it make sense to argue that might excludes right, and yet without it, the body politic lies in ruins.

Our problem in a nutshell. The 'two levels' contradict one another, and yet no state can function unless they co-exist. Even a theorist like Marx, who, it is often supposed, identifies politics purely with power, has to find space for the element of authority within his political definitions. Read Marx carefully, and what do you find? Politics is not merely the power of one class to oppress another. Political power has to be 'organised', and all organisation involves, as Plato's earlier comment reminds us, some unity of purpose even if this is no more than an honour among thieves. Political coercion is a force which is necessarily 'public' in character. To have 'official status' it must be socially recognised. This is why, for Marx, movements become political only when they possess a 'general, socially coercive force': a force which has to be acceptable in the eyes of society at large (Hoffman, 1984, pp. 18–19; p. 33). Force and legitimacy may constitute contradictory attributes within the political process but they are never far apart. Power has to evoke respect and recognition (i.e. enjoy authority) before it can become political.

Our problem can be tabulated as follows:

Power implies	*Authority implies*
coercion	consent
force	morality
subordination	will
dependence	autonomy

Each conceptual coupling expresses the problem of the 'two levels'. Both partners within the antinomy appear essential to politics, and yet each seemingly excludes the other. Contemporary political theorists have analysed the question of power and authority with a bewildering array of 'taxonomies' but, whatever the diversity of their definitions, in each case the problem of this contradictory relationship raises its head.

To take two examples. In his *Modern Political Analysis*, Dahl argues that while power and authority are both forms of influence, they can be distinguished only along a continuum. We begin with 'trained control', where people respond habitually to instruction. This is followed by 'rational persuasion' (where influence is exerted through a communication believed to be truthful); 'manipulative persuasion' (when the communication is deliberately deceptive); 'inducement' (where a reward is offered); and 'power' proper (where alongside the reward, a sanction is threated in the case of non-compliance). 'Coercion', for Dahl, arises when sanctions are threatened without any compensating inducement, and 'physical force' comes into play when a threat has to be enacted.

Dahl calls these distinctions 'differences that makes a difference', but what is not clear is whether the different forms of influence which range across Dahl's continuum can actually be separated out. They do not 'have crystalline boundaries'. They 'merge into one another' (1976, p. 42), and in the political process at any rate they form the contradictory components of a single identity.

To take a second example of the problem at hand. As far as Bachrach and Baratz are concerned, the contrast between power and authority needs to be rather more sharply drawn. Dahl's continuum is replaced by clusters of concepts around polar opposites. Dahl's 'rational persuasion' becomes a species of authority; his notion of coercion a form of power. The concept of 'trained control' is excluded from Bachrach and Baratz's analysis altogether on the grounds that the automatic acceptance of a command lacks the element of rationality necessary for authority relationships. Likewise, physical force is not considered a species of power; since power can be extercised by one person over another only when there is an element of choice involved. As for influence, this is not a generic term as it is in Dahl, but a relationship rather like Dahl's 'inducement' (1969, p. 105).

If the terminology and some of the argumentation is different, however, the problem is the same. Politics consists of a combination of two levels, each in sharp contradiction with the other. Our question therefore still stands: if power and authority are so different, why do they co-exist as warring factions within the realm of the state? How is it possible for *one* institution to contain two attributes in perpetual and radical conflict with one another?

Some theorists even see the problem of the two levels reproducing itself within each of the 'polar opposites'. Day argues (1963, p. 262), for example, that within the arena of authority, one might distinguish between a 'sociological' authority—which exists where society generally supports the acts of a government—and a 'legal' authority which arises when laws enjoy a purely formal recognition. Thus, during the years of prohibition in the USA, we could say that the law was legally authoritative but 'sociologically' disregarded, and thus lacked any real clout. And yet, as Day himself acknowledges, the two ultimately go together. Laws are unlikely to survive for long if the sociological basis for their 'legal authority' has disappeared. Authority has to be socially enforceable if it is to be more than a constitutional fiction.

In the same way even the most brutish kind of power has to secure compliance if its brutishness is to be effective, and compliance implies recognition of some kind. However we look at the problem of power and authority, the Machiavellian centaur continues to raise its head. There is a continual intermeshing of the two levels: they exist together, and yet each defines itself in opposition to the other.

This then is what we have called the problem of the contradictory relationship. To make sense of it, there is a further question which we must now to tackle.

THE PARTIES ARE INCOMPATIBLE: WHY NO DIVORCE?

A number of theorists take the view that although power and authority are often linked, they can be separated out as discrete political activities. Indeed, were this to prove possible, we could then answer our conundrum of the centaur in the following way.

Power and authority may be contradictory attributes of the political process, but this poses no conceptual difficulties since we can find one existing apart from the other. This means, so the argument might run, that although the state is usually defined as having a monopoly of legitimate violence, in fact some states can be violent without being legitimate, and others legitimate without being violent.

Establish this kind of separation, and our problem dissolves. Even if some states try to fuse the two levels together, there is no necessity for them to do so. Where politics rests on consent, it can avoid coercion, and where it resorts to coercion, it sacrifices the moral authority derived from consent. On this argument, politics is a common-sensical rather than a paradoxical process, and the relationship between power and authority, like the question of the state itself, becomes a simple matter of consistent definition. Classical writers, obsessed with centaurs and conundrums, contradictions and perplexing paradoxes, have been making a fuss over nothing.

But can power and authority be separated out quite as easily as 'common-sense' theorists suppose? We turn out to examine some of the arguments of those who favour an empirical cleavage—an actual institutional separation—between power and authority, in order to try to focus more precisely the problem before us.

In her *Authority and Democracy*, April Carter argues for a view of authority strict enough to differentiate it rigorously from power. Compliance with authority, she contends, must be voluntary. Not only must there be an absence of physical force, but there should be no psychological pressures either. A person obeys authority out of rational considerations. It is true that persuasion itself is not always necessary since a person can accept authority through habit. But if authority involves an automatic tendency to comply with commands, there must exist at the same time a readiness to question the reasons for, and the rightness of, decisions authoritatively accepted (1979, p. 80).

This means that whereas Dahl, for example (1976, p. 60), identifies authority with legitimacy, Carter argues that the two should be kept apart because legitimacy may well involve coercive and psychological pressures incompatible with the rational exercise of authority. Take Weber's three sources of legitimacy as a way of elaborating this point. Charisma or hero-worship invariably incorporates a good deal of deception, manipulation and fraud, and so embraces legitimacy as *opposed* to authority. Tradition implies a kind of habitual respect which does not normally involve the readiness to question decisions taken, while even the legitimacy of 'rational-legal' structures entails a capacity to 'impose discipline', and thus the use of coercive sanctions (1979, p. 27). As far as Carter is concerned then, governments may well be legitimate in the sense they enjoy widespread support, but to the extent that this support is either the product of or is used to justify coercive pressures it undermines authority.

It is not difficult to see how an argument like this over-reaches itself. If, as Carter contends, authority is not even a 'form of rule', then we are tempted to ask, what has it to do with politics? Carter tells us that in the political sphere, 'authority rarely exists in its pure form' (1979, p. 41). Even a constitutional government acting with great liberalism and tolerance would still lack 'pure authority' since 'it relies ultimately upon coercion' (1979, p. 33). Indeed Carter actually speaks of 'political authority' as a 'paradox'—a potential contradiction in terms. Where a voluntary acceptance of commonly agreed rules is most practicable, authority is least necessary. The existence of common values works to obviate major conflict so that no 'authorities' are needed to sort matters out (1979, p. 39). The familiar predicament noted by Rousseau in his analysis of the Lawgiver: governments are most likely to succeed where they are not really necessary.

But where does this leave Carter's search for a 'pure authority' devoid of power? By having to withdraw authority from the political process in order to protect it from a contaminating coercion, Carter can only reiterate (rather than resolve) the problem of the authority/power distinction. Pure authority, as far as politics is concerned, is a pure abstraction. The two levels may be mutually antagonistic but it is no easy task to separate them meaningfully.

Lukes, however, in a classic work on the subject, contends that it is possible to identify a 'consensual behaviour' which involves authority but no power. He cites the arguments of Hannah Arendt and Talcott Parsons to make his point. Their only problem, he says, is a terminological one. They speak of power when they ought really to refer to authority, but both theorists are able to demonstrate the possibility of separating out in an empirical way our two Gramscian levels.

Arendt quotes Madison: 'all governments rest on opinion' (Lukes, 1974, p. 29). The concept of power (or in our terminology here, authority) is tied to a tradition which can be traced back to Athens and Rome, where the republic is based on the rule of law—the 'power of the people'. This 'power' must be dissociated from 'the command-obedience relationship' and the business of dominion, for power is consensual. It enjoys a legitimacy which violence can never attain. 'Power and violence are opposites; where the one rules absolutely, the other is absent' (Lukes, 1974, p. 30).

Talcott Parsons, Lukes tells us, takes a similar position. Power (or again, as we would say, authority) involves the use of authoritative decisions to further collective goals: A has power over B when he or she has the right to make decisions which take precedence in the 'interest of the effectiveness of the collective operation as a whole' (1974, p. 28). Power therefore is tied to consensus and the pursuit of collective goals: it is divorced, Luke concludes, from conflicts of interest, coercion and force.

But it is by no means clear that Arendt and Parsons are attempting to drive an empirical wedge between power and authority in the way Lukes suggest. Take Arendt's argument that 'even the most despotic domination we know of', the rule of masters over slaves, does not rest on 'superior means of coercion as such, but on a superior organisation of power—that is on the organised solidarity of the masters' (Lukes, 1974, p. 30). This example provides no help at all to Lukes's argument that power and authority can be spliced apart, since Arendt is not saying that masters ruled over slaves in a way which involved authority without coercion. She is merely insisting that that the relationship did not rest on 'coercion as such'.

Power, she implies, rests upon a combination of coercion and consent. No government exclusively based on the means of violence has ever existed (Arendt, 1970, p. 50), so that her criticisms are directed against those who imagine that power rests upon force alone. Likewise there is nothing in her example of the 'despotic domination' of masters over slaves to suggest that a political relationship can rest on 'pure consent' since she explicitly states that nothing is less frequent than to find either violence or what she calls power in their pure forms (1970, p. 45). Indeed her somewhat idiosyncratic use of the term 'power' captures the problem of the 'two levels' quite well, although it certainly does not solve it.

In the case of Parsons, Lukes's misunderstanding is even more straightforward. Parsons makes it clear that power involves the performance of 'binding obligations' in the pursuit of collective goals. In the case of 'recalcitrance', therefore, there is a presumption of the 'enforcement of negative situational sanctions' (1974, p. 28). Clearly then Parsons is not, as Lukes contends, seeking to dissociate power from force since 'binding obligations' and 'negative situational sanctions' manifestly imply an element of coercion. Indeed Parsons insists that both the coercive and consensual aspects of politics are essential to an analysis of power (1969, p. 251). This is why he argues that the threat of coercive measures 'without legitimation or justification' should not properly be called the use of power, for power requires an 'institutional code' through which it is organised and legitimised (1969, p. 263).

It is hard to see therefore how the two levels can exist apart. 'Pure' force must always be exercised in conjunction with authority. Why else does Arendt speak of the 'despotic domination' of masters over slaves, or Parsons insist that binding obligations require 'negative situational sanctions'? The problem facing us then is this. Only a naive autocrat imagines that politics can exist without morality, opinion, persuasion and consent. On the other hand, if power and authority are not the 'same thing', it must be possible to distinguish them. The question is how?

We might argue in response to the difficulties noted above that only an analytical distinction between power and authority is possible: a real-life divorce is not. But this does not really solve our problem, for if power and authority *can't* be distinguished in the real world, then how can they be distinguished at all? If an empirical distinction is impossible, then what is the basis for supposing that we can make an analytical one?

The problem brings us back once again to the state. As long as power and authority centre on the state's monopoly of legitimate force, then whatever analytical refinements we propose, the paradoxical qualities of the political process will inevitably reproduce themselves in the contradictory relationship between power and authority. No matter how vigorously we assert their incompatibility, nothing seems able to effect a divorce.

We turn therefore to another line of argument in our search for a solution.

CAN A SOCIAL ANALYSIS UNLOCK THE EMBRACE?

It is perhaps significant that those theorists who believe that it is possible to divorce power from authority tend to examine the question in a context wider than the state. Lukes, for example, appears to analyse power in terms of a broad social view of the political process, taking as his exemplar of the power relationship, exchanges between A and B, where A and B may simply be relating individuals. True, he does not exclude the state from his analysis but he gives it no particular emphasis, and, as we have already seen, argues that a non-coercive authority is possible where no conflict is involved.

Dahl's position here is an interesting one. He also adopts, as we noted in the previous section, a broad social view of the political process and, as we have seen, in his chapter on the 'forms of influence' he provides a detailed analysis of 'differences which make a difference'. The question therefore arises: does Dahl's non-statist view of politics facilitate the attempt to disentangle the intermeshing skein of our contradictory relationship? Like Lukes (1974, pp. 33–4), Dahl wonders whether rational persuasion in politics should be treated as a form of power when it lies at the heart of so many conceptions of an ideal society. Is it possible for politics to rely upon persuasion alone? Theorists like Rousseau speak of morally free citizens who are bound only by laws of their own choosing, and the notion of politics as persuasion is central to much democratic and anarchist thought (1976, p. 51).

Yet despite his 'social' view of politics, Dahl finds that a divorce between power and authority can exist only under impossibly idealised conditions. The sad fact is that manipulative persuasion, power, coercion, the threat and application of physical force are all 'commonplace' (and it would seem, interpenetrating) aspects of political life. In many parts of the world today, civil strife, violence, revolutions, the forceful suppression of political opponents are 'normal' political practices. Just suppose a people were prepared to govern themselves through rational persuasion alone, and in this way secure an absolute divorce between power and authority. What would happen, Dahl asks, if no one else followed suit? Unless universally adopted, such a solution would 'immediately lead to self-contradiction'.

It is also worth remembering, Dahl argues, that rational persuasion for some can mean coercion for others. In 1787 the Founding Fathers agreed to a new constitution for the United States which at the same time perpetuated and confirmed the existence of slavery in the South. Dahl might have also cited here Rousseau's reference to the way in which the ancient Greeks were able to meet continuously in the market place in order to resolve their differences through rational persuasion. Is freedom to be maintained only with the support of slavery? Rousseau asks. 'Perhaps. The two extremes meet' (1968, pp. 142–3). What is persuasion for one may be servitude for another. Islands of 'authority' presuppose a surrounding sea of power.

Dahl is therefore gloomy. What these examples show, he argues, is not that coercion is necessarily justifiable but the tragic dilemma which the citizen must face. One may not face this dilemma responsibly but no one has yet discovered a way to avoid it. The continued existence of both power and authority, rational persuasion and physical force in politics is 'one of the most poignant and troubling problems' of social and political life (1976, p. 53).

As far as Dahl is concerned then, a broad social view of politics does not really help. But it may well be argued that this is because Dahl does not actually exclude the state from his political analysis: he merely seeks to go beyond it. The state (or Government as he calls it) does after all represent one kind of political system, and most if not all of the negative examples he cites against the exercise of pure authority do in fact involve the state. What would happen, however, if we sought to eliminate the state entirely from our analysis? If we adopted an explicitly social, and not just a broadly political view of the authority/power relationship?

While Carter, for example, is doubtful about finding authority without power in the context of the state, she has little difficulty in providing what she believes are everyday *social* examples of pure authority at work. What of the relationship, she asks, between teacher and student, doctor and patient, parent and child? Are these not spheres in which we witness the kind of habitual respect which is essential for authority but which excludes power (1979, p. 70)? And even when we take examples of social institutions (like trade unions) which do exercise a co-operative social power, this is, Carter insists, a kind of power which does not (or need not) involve coercion.

Taylor argues for a similar position. True, he concedes, not all coercion comes from the state. Even stateless societies may employ coercion in creating social order. The crucial point, however, is that they *need* not. A society without any form of coercion at all is 'conceivable' (1982, p. 25). As Taylor sees it, this possibility arises through the distinction he makes between threats and offers in his analysis of power. While threats involve coercion, 'offers' do not. The two may of course exist together (as 'throffers') but here Taylor follows Nozick. It is quite possible for someone to make an offer simply on its own—a proposal, the consequences of which makes things better for the person who complies. Since a rational individual can be expected to welcome such 'offers', it would be inappropriate to call them coercive.

Take Nozick's example of the butcher who increases the price of meat in line with the general run of price increases elsewhere. This cannot be seen as an activity which is coercive even if, says Taylor, an unfair or exploitative exchange between buyer and seller was involved (1982, p. 18). For power to be coercive, it must involve a substantial and credible threat.

This 'Nozickian' analysis is particularly interesting because it raises the whole question of the market as a non-coercive mechanism. It has important implications for exploring the power/authority relationship since, as far as New Right theorists like Norman Barry are concerned, the exchange of the free market provide everyday examples of authority without power. While it is of the essence of power relationships that they involve the diminution of liberty, 'this is not the normal characteristic of exchange' (1981, p. 72). People who exchange goods and services in the free market can be said to exercise their will autonomously. Even though the wider framework of the state is necessary to underpin this exchange process, here at least, it is argued, we can find social relationships which manifest an authority without power.

Nor, it should be noted, is this argument advanced only by thinkers of the New Right. We have already seen Nozick's position endorsed by Taylor, a left-wing anarchist. Support, albeit of a somewhat more qualified kind, can also be found for this analysis of the market in the work of the New Left theorist, C.B. Macpherson. In a critical assessment of Milton Friedman's *Capitalism and Freedom*, Macpherson challenges the argument that exchanges in a capitalist society are free and voluntary. The existence, he argues, of a labour force which lacks sufficient capital to work for themselves, constitutes a denial of choice: the choice as to whether to enter into exchange relations or not. 'Where there is no choice, there is coercion' (1973, p. 146). If exploitative classes exist, then power and not merely authority is involved.

But there is one set of circumstances which would seem to vindicate the libertarian argument of the New Right. Take the simple market model where very household has *enough* either to produce goods and services for itself, or to exchange with others. In this situation the decision to exchange arises freely, out of choice: an example, says Macpherson, of co-operation without coercion (1973, p. 145). It may well be that simple market models are rather more difficult to find in the real world than complex capitalist ones, but as far as Macpherson is concerned, it is at least possible to stipulate the kind of social conditions which make (in our terms) authority without power possible.

This whole line of argument, however, runs into an acute difficulty. It is true that the problem of the Machiavellian centaur arises specifically in the context of the state, which, through its monopoly of legitimate force, yokes together our two incompatible concepts. It might be thought, therefore, that once we move away from the concentrated power of the state, we can identify autonomous individuals able to relate to one another in an authentically 'authoritative' way, either through teacher/pupil, doctor/patient relationships, or through free market exchanges. Relief at last from those tragic dilemmas and perplexing paradoxes of power and authority that arise in the context of the state! Just as classical liberals first tackled the question of individual freedom in the abstract before turning to the problem of the 'social contract', so, it might be argued, we too can establish our own islands of authority in acts of autonomous individuality before moving on to make sense of the legitimate power of the state.

But here is the rub. The state, as we have seen, merely concentrates the relationships which exist in society at large. If power and authority are fused together in the concentrated agencies of the state, why should they mysteriously fall apart in the informal world of social relationships? The classical liberals, of course, postulated an authoritative autonomy for private individuals by abstracting them from society itself (and not merely from the state); but even the most enthusiastic libertarian today shrinks back (as we noted in our previous section) from outright mystification of this kind. Once individuals are seen as social beings, for better or for worse, it is far from clear that private activities can provide the solution to public problems. So our question remains: why should society exhibit an empirical separation between power and authority when that divide appears nowhere to be found when we analyse the legitimate force of the state?

As we have already seen, the most common-sensical examples of theory in practice can be quite misleading. If the state is paradoxical in the way it concentrates power, is not this because social relationships themselves have a contradictory character? The divorce between power and authority is rather more elusive than our social analysts imagine, and nowhere do we see this more clearly than in an argument about power which began in the late 1950s. Almost thirty years later it shows no signs of abating.

5 The Dimensions Debate and the Problem of Structure

THE PLURALIST CASE FOR THE DISPERSAL OF POWER

The relationship between power and authority appears impossibly contradictory as long as we analyse it in the context of the 'legitimate force' of the state. Many contend, however, that in the diffuse and informal world of social relationships, a real separation between power and authority is possible. But does a purely social analysis of the problem really offer a way out?

We turn now to consider what it is convenient to call (with a little help from Lukes) the 'dimensions debate', the argument over the nature of power which Robert Dahl (and his team of researchers) initiated in 1961, and which still continues to reverberate. This debate offers insights into the conundrum of Machiavelli's centaur which are startling and unexpected. They are insights, as we shall see, that radically call into question the whole classical liberal perception of power and authority—a perception which, it goes without saying, still exercises a remarkable hold over political theory up to the present day.

On the surface of things, it would seem that a foray into the dimensions debate would help the social analysts in their attempts to separate power and authority. It is true that Dahl himself, as we have noted, is sceptical that such a separation is possible despite his social view of the political process. His classic work *Who Governs?* sets out, however, to analyse the question of power in a local rather than a national context, and his argument has a distinctly anti-statist flavour. If the state with its stress on monopoly and concentration, appears to suggest a national division between the haves and have-nots, an analysis of politics at the local level points to a much more pluralistic distribution of power in which the emphasis falls upon bargaining rather than hierarchy; upon consensus rather than coercion.

Dahl's book is a sustained attack on what he has called (elsewhere) 'the lump of power fallacy' (1976, p. 26)—the idea that if one group has power, others have none. This is a fallacy which arises, Dahl argues, because quite different kinds of power and influence are crudely lumped together on the assumption, for example, that if people have wealth, they will also have status, and if they have status, they will automatically command popular support.

Who Governs? radically challenges these contentions. It focusses in depth on the politics of New Haven (the city where Dahl's own University of Yale is situated), and questions the assumption made by so many classical writers that the equality of social conditions is a necessary prerequisite for the equality of power (1961, p. 3). Of course, Dahl accepts that New Haven is a very unequal city in terms of ownership of property and distribution of wealth, the spread of educational attainment and symbols of status. Nevertheless he sets out to demonstrate that in New Haven (and by implication throughout Western liberal society as a whole) these inequalities are 'dispersed' so that it can be said (in answer to the question which the book poses) that 'no one' actually governs at all, at least not in any kind of exclusive or monopolistic way. The pluralist society, in other words, relies much more upon authority than it does upon force.

Dahl's book is a behaviouralist classic. Given the instructive nature of the controversy which it has provoked, it is worth examining its arguments in some detail. Dahl's decision to focus in depth on the politics of one city was motivated by the view that this would make a rigorous and methodologically sophisticated analysis of power possible, and, as we shall see, his analysis throws crucial (if unintended) light onto the power/authority conundrum.

The work seeks to show that those who claim that power is

always concentrated in a single elite or ruling class have a problem not with their values, but with their facts. A detailed sample survey of registered voters, leaders and sub-leaders serves to rebut slipshod and unsubstantiated argument by making it possible to idenitify clearly those who actually exercise power. Indeed, in his earlier critique of the 'ruling elite' model, Dahl insists that an analysis of power can be meaningful only if the group allegedly monopolising power is clearly defined; if the decisions through which they exercise their power are explicitly identified; and if the issues in which they have influence are specifically pin-pointed (1969, p. 39). Far too often, analysts of power simply assume that having a 'reputation' for power or commanding substantial amounts of wealth is in itself an adequate indicator of a ruling elite, or they mistakenly imagine that because individuals are influential in one area of political life, they are necessarily influential in others.

At the heart of *Who Governs?* is the argument that if power is to be identified empirically and scientifically, then it must be identified as decision making. Those who have power are those who either make or break decisions, and hence a study of power is first and foremost an analysis of the decision-makers. This is why the book opens with an examination of the social background of New Haven's mayors, and contends that their changing social background (from bankers to businessmen to lower-middle-class immigrants) signals the declining importance of wealth and status in the city's politics. With the extension of the franchise and the competitive party system, the capacity of leaders from a humble background to command popular support becomes a vital and separate 'resource' in acquiring power.

But what of the argument that the wealthy and the well connected may have ceased to be political leaders taking decisions, but they continue to exercise power from behind the scenes? To tackle this objection, Dahl shifts his focus beyond leadership at the mayoral level, and analyses the occupants of all the key offices in his three designated issue areas—the nomination of candidates for public office; public education (the costliest item in the city's budget); and New Haven's urban redevelopment programme (the largest in the country).

Those with wealth and status, the city's Economic and Social Notables (ENs and SNs) occupy, Dahl finds, a trivial proportion of the hundreds of offices which govern these three issue areas alone. In most cases the ENs are more influential than the SNs (Dahl treats them as two separate categories with very little overlap), but only in the area of urban re-development do the two together hold around ten per cent of the offices. Hardly enough to suggest that a socio-economic elite has some kind of covert monopoly of power.

If we focus on the top fifty decision-makers, we find that less than half of them are ENs and SNs. If we expand our numbers to take account of sub-leaders, we find that only a tiny percentage of these leaders are influential in more than one issue area. True, sub-leaders tend to be men rather than women, and hold white-collar rather than blue-collar jobs but it is still noteworthy that different issue areas attract sub-leaders from different social backgrounds. Leaders from upper-working-class strata are more likely to be involved in nominating candidates for public office; those from upper-middle-class background more inclined to take part in the urban redevelopment programme. Again, Dahl argues, the evidence suggests a spread rather a concentration of power.

Of all the decision-makers Dahl analyses, only the mayor has any real overall power, but this does nothing to help the ruling-class or ruling-elite thesis. The leadership patterns, as Dahl calls them, do not involve a 'covert integration' of influence but constant negotiation, bargaining and compromise. Thus the mayor can find himself defeated by rival coalitions or be forced to substantially modify decisions already taken as a result of counter-pressures. He has some power but so do many others.

For this, Dahl insists, is the point. Different people have different amounts of power in different areas. Difference politicians utilise different resources—money and credit; control over jobs; ownership and control of the media; social status; charisma and popularity—with different degrees of efficacy. Hence the possession of political skill is yet *another* factor which must be weighed in the balance. Unequal as all these factors are, the inequalities which they generate are necessarily 'dispersed'. Power is spread among different people with different interests, skills, social backgrounds and areas of involvement.

While Dahl is sceptical, as we have already seen, about the practicality of a radical divorce between coercive power and moral authority in political life, his pluralistic system rests upon (and also helps to generate) a high degree of ideological consensus: political leaderships enjoy substantial legitimacy on the basis of a widely shared democratic creed.

This then is the substance of Dahl's celebrated case for the pluralist dispersal of power. By focussing upon decision-making as the activity through which power must be identified and analysed, Dahl believes that it is possible to present an empirically rigorous and theoretically plausible proof for the pluralist case. His thesis is highly novel, and it is scarcely an exaggeration to say it set the tone for much of the post-war political theorising on power in the Anglo-American world. Nevertheless, for all its ingenuity, his thesis is also vulnerable, and as we probe its problems, we will begin to see what bearing the pluralist case has on the contradictory relationship between power and authority.

INDIRECT INFLUENCE AND THE EROSION FROM WITHIN

Dahl's thesis has attracted a substantial body of criticism over the years, and in what is perhaps one of the most stimulating critiques of *Who Governs?*, Lukes contends that Dahl's whole approach is superficial and unsatisfactory. In Lukes's view, power should be analysed in a 'three-dimensional' way: Dahl's conceptualisations suffer from 'one-dimensionality'. His attempt to analyse power simply in terms of decision-making is constricting, and poses major dilemmas for the pluralist thesis.

To get to grips with the Lukes critique, we need to remember that the analysis of power as decision-making was first explored, not by pluralists, but by the champions of elite theory. Writers like Pareto, Mosca and Michels were all hostile to pluralism because they believed that power was always and of necessity concentrated in the hands of an elite. Popular government was an absurd abstraction; rule by an elite the permanent feature of government in all its forms. The elite theorists found the analysis of power as decision-making most congenial. Since it could be shown without difficulty that governmental decisions are invariably taken by a few, this kind of analysis demonstrated therefore that power itself is always highly concentrated.

The decision-making approach also appears in the work of right-wing German theorists in the 1920s. As a result, one behaviouralist comments rather gingerly that careful investigation is needed 'to determine the extent to which the current approach to decision-making resembles this earlier theory'. Since the analysis by German theorists was 'subsequently used to bolster the Nazi regime', any similarity would have to be taken into account in a final evaluation of this concept (Easton, 1950, p. 472). It was therefore a matter of some embarrasment in the 1950s that a concept which had been central to traditional elite theory should now be employed in the case for pluralism.

But why should the decision-making concept pose problems for Dahl? Dahl, as we have seen, places great emphasis upon the diversity of interests and resources among decision-makers, and upon their heterogeneous social background. The whole drift of his analysis is away from the idea that power is concentrated. Yet the truth is that Dahl cannot deny that those who actually *take* decisions are relatively few in number. There exists in political life, he comments, 'a small stratum of individuals' who are 'much more highly involved in political thought, discussion and action, than the rest of the population' (1961, p. 90).

In these three issue areas he selects for analysis, a small number of leading figures take all the decisions. It may be that nominations for public office require the support of registered voters who attend primaries. But these occasions are largely ceremonial and ritualistic in character—'not unlike the traditional tribal rites prescribed for warriors before battle' (1961, p. 113)—and the whole nomination process might well be seen as the 'creation and instrumentality of the leaders' (1961, p. 106). It is true that the mayor and his urban redevelopment team are accountable to a 400-strong Citizens

Action Commission but this body has never been known to initiate, veto or alter any proposal from the mayor and his development administrator. It is hard therefore not to conclude that in its origin, conception and execution, the whole urban redevelopment programme was 'the direct product of a small handful of leaders' (1961, p. 115). Likewise, in public education. Wider bodies like parent Teacher Associations simply furnish loyal 'auxiliaries' for administrators, who take the key decisions.

All this would seem to put Dahl's thesis in a rather different light. We are reliably informed that 'only a small group of citizens' participate steadily in the political process, using their political resources at a high rate, and in this way exerting a 'very high degree of influence' (1961, p. 301). Most people are simply not interested. To them, politics is a remote, alien and unrewarding activity best left to the professionals. This then is Dahl's dilemma. To have power, you must get involved in making decisions. This is why shadowy groups who allegedly manipulate things from afar are disqualified from consideration. No decision-making; no power. So what are we to say when the facts show that very few people actually take any decisions, even in political systems which are apparently pluralistic in character?

Moreover it needs to be remembered that the elite thesis as it was classically conceived could embrace at least 'elements' of pluralism. Gaetano Mosca in the later editions of his *Ruling Class* argued the case for reciprocal controls among differing elites, and stressed the importance of opening the ranks of the elite to forces from below. But this was not an argument for genuine pluralism: it was a plea (Mosca, 1939, p. 493) for an elite ruling class to exercise greater political competence and understanding!

The decision-making thesis, in other words, cuts both ways. The same empirical rigour which demonstrates that Dahl's ENs and SNs hold very few offices, also points inexorably to the fact that only a tiny portion of the population are involved in taking decisions anyway. If there is diversity of interest and heterogeneity of background, it is confined to the ranks of a small elite.

Dahl concedes that there is a problem. 'It is easy to see', he writes, 'why observers have often pessimistically concluded that the internal dynamics of political associations create forces alien to popular control' (1961, p. 100). At the same time, to endorse such a conclusion would be irreparably damaging to the pluralist thesis. Accordingly, Dahl argues as follows. While it is true that a few persons have a great deal of *direct* influence over decisions which are made, most citizens exercise an *indirect* influence over those who make them. Leaders need to win elections; they have constituents who comprise most of the adult population; these constituents can vote without intimidation or bribery, and they are informed about the policies presented to them by competing candidates. Under these conditions it is possible to argue that if the leaders lead, they are also led—a 'stubborn and pervasive ambiguity' permeates the entire political system (1961, p. 102).

Thus if we return briefly to Dahl's three issue areas. The registered voters who attend election primaries or the ordinary voters to take part in elections may not choose candidates for public office, but party leaders will nevertheless have to take their views into account by selecting candidates with electoral appeal. The mayor in implementing the urban redevelopment programme needs to anticipate the possible reaction of his Citizens Action Commission and the wider electorate to the decisions he makes. Likewise with the education administrators: they need to enjoy the confidence of the teachers and the voters if they are to govern effectively. In each case, it can be said that individuals who seem to have the greatest influence are themselves influenced by 'the need to gain and retain popular support' (1961, p. 155). This is the ambiguity of leadership. A few may take all the decisions but most have *indirect* influence. The decision-makers have to take them into account.

This is a plausible and interesting response to the 'elite' argument. It breathes new life into the pluralist case but at the same time places a depth charge into the foundations of Dahl's concept of power. For Dahl can salvage his pluralism only by severing the link between power and decision-making since, as Lukes is quick to point out, the thesis that indirect influence gives the electorate control over leaders 'can be turned on its head' (1974, p. 37). What is sauce for the goose is sauce for the gander. The indirect influence which enables electors to constrain leaders in office also enables other informal groups to exercise a veto power. If electors can exercise power without formally making decisions, why not ENs and SNs? As Crenson has pointed out (1970, p. 55), if indirect influence can work for ordinary citizens, why can't it also work for US Steel, General Motors, bank presidents or the members of a social elite?

Dahl's concept of indirect influence points to what two of his early critics, Bachrach and Baratz, call 'the politics of non-decision-making'. This is the kind of informal pressure which causes politicians to confine the scope of decision-making to relatively 'safe' issues (Lukes, 1974, p. 18). Just how 'informal' this kind of pressure can be, is indicated by Dahl's willingness to extend the concept of indirect influence to that of *potential* influence, for 'potential influence' is something which people can enjoy even they don't actually do anything at all! A person who exercises potential influence may not even vote. All that needs to exist is the possibility that at some point in future he or she may wish to become politically involved. It is to avoid the translation of a potential into an indirect influence that politicians feel obliged to expand the numbers of people whose wishes they have to take into account.

But this kind of argument is highly congenial to 'ruling-class' analysis. Indeed Dahl himself gives a good example of how his ENs and SNs can utilise the same kind of indirect and potential influence which he ascribes to the active and passive members of the electorate. The ENs, in particular, Dahl tells us, are strongly opposed to increasing taxes and expanding the public services, so much so that 'a city administration lives in dread of raising the tax rate' (1961, p. 81). Hence, we are told, 'politicians are wary of their potential influence and avoid policies that might unite the Notables in bitter opposition' (1961, p. 84).

This is a revealing point. After all, wealthy business people do not even have to threaten to withdraw their investments or sack their workers in order to bring the local city authorities into line. The fact that the political leaders perceive the *potential* of the business community for bringing this kind of pressure to bear is enough to make them respectfully 'wary'. So why aren't the SNs and ENs a good example of a ruling class, of a politically influential socio-economic elite?

It is true that their interests are highly specific. But this in itself is also more revealing that Dahl supposes. After all, we would not expect ENs and SNs to be interested in the administration of public education when they send their children to private schools, or to bother with *inner-city* nominations for public office when they live in the suburbs. The urban redevelopment programme, on the other hand, is something which does interest them, and we will return to this issue later. So is the issue of local government finances but this is an issue which, astonishingly, Dahl does not even select for special consideration. The provision of finances is not just 'one issue' among many. It is a *key* one since it affects all the others. If the Board of Finance is constrained (as Dahl himself admits) by the indirect and potential influence of ENs and SNs, this is surely a fact of central significance.

Dahl's dilemma then is this. In order to prevent his pluralist case from sliding into an admission that a handful of decision-makers constitute a power elite, he introduces the concept of indirect and potential influence. But this, as we have seen, has the effect of undermining his analysis of power as decision-making, and thus serves to sabatoge earlier arguments against the covert influence or socio-economic elites. This is the difficulty that Dahl now has to tackle.

THE PROBLEM OF CONSENSUS AND POWER

The concepts of indirect and potential influence may deflect attention away from the problem of decision-makers as a minority, but they make the ruling-class thesis—that power is concentrated in the hands of a socio-economic elite—all the more plausible as a result. How is Dahl to avoid jumping out of the frying pan into the fire?

Dahl concedes that his conceptual innovations would prove troublesome for the pluralist case were it not for the fact that the attitudes adopted by the ENs and SNs are basically the same as those of everyone else. New Haven is a polity in which a wide-ranging *consensus* prevails. Even the socialists in New Haven are so 'economy-minded' that they command the respect (if not the votes) of Republican businessmen! The consensus is one to which all the major groups in the community subscribe. There is nothing therefore particularly significant about the likes and dislikes of the notables, and there is no reason to believe that they exert a disproportionate or 'sinister' influence over the politicians.

Take the case of John Golden, New Haven's Democratic Party leader for a generation. It might be thought that because Golden was an insurance executive and bank director, he would be especially sympathetic to the ENs. It is true, Dahl says, that the views of Golden and the business community did not significantly diverge but so what? Golden's views did not diverge from other sections of the community either—'union leaders, school teachers and factory hands' (1961, p. 75). The existence of a consensus between political leaders and the community as a whole neutralises the elitist implications which might otherwise flow from the concepts of indirect and potential influence. If everyone supports the interests of business and banking, why pick on the ENs?

Again, an ingenious argument but one which obliges Dahl to move even further away from his behavioural concept of power. In his original critique of the ruling elite model, Dahl had insisted that power must not only manifest itself through decision-making, but it must do so also in a situation in which two or more groups disagree over these decisions, Unless one group exercises its preference in *opposition* to another, how can we sure that it has any real power? In a situation of consensus, there is 'no conceivable way of determining who is ruler and who is ruled' (1969, p. 40).

This point of course creates a real problem for Dahl. In each of three issues which he selects for analysis in *Who Governs?* there is consensus rather than conflict between the decision-makers and the other groups in the community. Perhaps this is why Dahl proceeds to modify his earlier definition of power. A rough test of a person's overt or covert influence, he now asserts, includes not merely the frequency with which he or she initiates policies against the opposition of others or vetoes the policies initiated by another. Power may also be identified in cases where a person 'initiates a policy where no opposition appears' (1961, p. 66). This statement is in stark contrast to the earlier stress on observable conflict and, as Lukes comments, it is one of a number of examples in *Who Governs?* where the text is 'more subtle and profound' than the general conceptual and methodological pronouncements of its author (1974, p. 14). The 'consensus' argument is intended to rectify problems arising from the concept of indirect and potential influence. In fact, it makes Dahl's attempt to establish a pluralist dispersal of power look little more than a pious gesture.

According to Dahl, as we have seen, the ENs and SNs of New Haven do not constitute an elite, because the belief system of the community itself has not 'at least so far' generated demands for local policies markedly antagonistic to the goals of the notables. But what would happen if conflict of this kind did develop? This, Dahl concedes, is not 'easy to predict' but judging from the fate of the patricians in New Haven in the nineteenth century, 'competitive politics would lead in the end to the triumph of numbers over Notability' (1961, p. 84).

This is, however (as Dahl the methodologist should be the first to acknowledge), sheer speculation, and in fact the contrast which Dahl draws between competitive politics and patrician rule in the first part of his book is much less con-clusive than he assumes. Dahl recalls how the patrician period saw sharp cleavages between Federalists and Democrats, so much so that the bitterness of the contention 'must have covered the small town like a dank fog' (1961, p. 19). In other words, it would seem that competitive politics *can* be compatible with 'patrician oligarchy'. The same is also true of consensus. The elite in the early days of New Haven, Dahl says, seems to have possessed that most indispensable of all characteristics in a dominant group, 'the sense, shared not only by themselves, but by the populace, that their claim to govern was legitimate' (1961, p. 17).

This raises a most telling point. If consensus and elite rule can co-exist, why can't a consensus be the creation of an elite? If there is no manifest conflict between rulers and ruled, then this surely must be deemed a possibility. It gives an added depth to what Lukes calls the two-dimensional argument about non decision-making, for it suggests that a 'shared belief system' which raises some issues for debate but suppresses others may itself be the product of elite rule.

Indeed this is the thrust of Domhoff's *Who Really Rules?*—a detailed and highly critical riposte to Dahl's *Who Governs?* For Domhoff shows how, for instance, the issue of urban redevelopment in Dahl's argument can be analysed as a classic example of ruling-class 'nondecision-making' in which business interests succeed in presenting a potentially divisive question in deceptively bland and uncontroversial terms.

The details of the Domhoff case cannot really concern us here, but suffice it to say that Domhoff looks beyond the local context of New Haven, and argues that the issue of urban development must be analysed in terms of the wider national argument about housing and profit that has taken place in the post-war period. Business interests favoured high-rise office buildings, tax-free auditoriums and luxury apartments: social liberals wanted subsidised housing. In New Haven, plans for urban redevelopment were shelved until Federal funding for the 'right' kind of construction became more readily available. Dahl's ENs had a very active interest in the development programme, and they demonstrated this interest not by initiating or vetoing decisions on the Citizens Action Commission, but by keeping the national debate over 'low cost housing' out of the politics of New Haven. The consensus around urban redevelopment which Dahl considered to be 'natural', was in fact contrived. It was an expression of elite or ruling-class power (Domhoff, 1978, p. 43 and *passim*).

The question of consensus does not therefore really help Dahl. It extricates him from one difficulty only by plunging him into another, and one even more intractable than the last. For it was Dahl himself who had earlier insisted that the existence of a political consensus makes it impossible to test the ruling-elite thesis one way or the other (1969, p. 40). And yet, if this methodological stance clearly makes things awkward for the pluralists, as we have just seen, it also makes things difficult for their critics as well.

The problem is basically this. In a situation of consensus, there is no observable conflict of interest through which to analyse decision-making. But if there is no overt activity to observe, how can one say anything meaningful about the process of nondecision-making either? How is it possible tackle the question of power in any one or in all three of its

Lukesian dimensions (in a consensus situation) when, on the surface of it, nothing happens?

This problem, as we shall now see, brings us right up against the troubled relationship between power and authority.

STRUCTURES AND AGENTS OF THE WORLD UNITE!

The behavioural view of power is seen by Lukes as 'one-dimensional' in character because it seeks to analyse the exercise of power as an observable activity—as decision-making. To the extent that other 'dimensions' are brought into the picture, the focus shifts away from observable action to the question of context or structure. Individual intention becomes less important as political leaders find themselves constrained by the collective exercise of indirect and potential influence, and by the impersonal existence of a social consensus. Increasingly, power has to be analysed through a prism of social patterning. We are concerned not so much with what particular individuals do (or what they intend) as we are with the existence of collectivities whose mere presence has an impact on the distribution of power.

This movement, however, beyond a one-dimensional view of power brings with it serious methodological problems. For if, as the critics of behaviouralism insist, power involves issues which never enter public debate, or decisions which are *not* taken, how is the exercise of this power to be identified? If power expresses itself through a variety of 'non-events', then an infinite number of hypothetical possibilities would seem to arise. Which one do we choose? There *might*, for example, have been a conflict between New Haven's Board of Finance and its elected politicians but for the potential influence of a seemingly uninvolved business elite. Yet how do we know? There *might* have been an outcry by the electors against the urban redevelopment plan, had it not appeared a purely consensus matter. But again the point is that nothing like this actually happened.

In practice, therefore, argue the pluralists, it will be the analysts, and not the people, who choose the issues which have been supposedly suppressed by a nondecision-making and consensus-forging elite. Since there are no actual observable activities to provide the investigator with a reliable guide as to which issues have been shut out, free reign can be given to personal preference—to private ideologies parading themselves with conceptual airs and graces in the name of con-textual power. This, in essence, is the pluralist reply to those who complain of a superficial one-dimensionality in the behavioural analysis of power (Lukes, 1974, pp. 38–9).

It is to meet objections like these that some of Dahl's critics accept that power must identified as an observable activity. This activity need not, however, involve formal decision-making. Thus Bachrach and Baratz contend that what they call nondecision-making is still an activity in its own right, even if it is the kind of activity which keeps issues off agendas and limits the scope of decisions. But how can we identify it?

There must, in the view of Bachrach and Baratz, at least be evidence of social and political conflict. This need not be the proceduralised conflict of a decision-making forum. Riots, demonstrations, protests, etc. are all examples of the kind of conflict which arises when one section of the community is left out in the cold as the victim of elitist nondecison-making. But what if, as in Dahl's *Who Governs?*, there is no conflict at all—there is merely consensus?

Here the advocates of the 'two-dimensional' position simply revert to a quasi-behavioural stance. No conflict: no non-decision-making. Unless nondecision-making can be empirically identified as some kind of *overt* activity, there can be no elite power. Where consensus prevails, it is simply impossible to make any critical assessment of the structure of power, for there are no analytical tools available which enable an investigator to determine whether a consensus is 'genuine', or whether it has in some way been manipulatively contrived (Lukes, 1974, pp. 19–20).

As far as Lukes is concerned, this 'two-dimensional' critique stops half-way, Bachrach and Baratz's analysis of racial tensions in Baltimore is a case in point. It suffers from superficiality because by confining itself to observable activity, it ignores the complex and subtle ways in which the *inactivity* of leaders, and the sheer weight of institutions left the black population in US cities relatively powerless in the 1960s. It is necessary, therefore, to think of the exercise or 'extertion' of power in collective and institutional terms, and not simply as the result of one individual intentionally and explicitly controlling another. The 'bias' of a system may itself privilege some and disadvantage others. In this it is sustained by what Lukes calls 'the socially structured and culturally patterned behaviour of groups, and practices of institutions' (1974, p. 22). This, in a word, is what constitutes the three-dimensional view of power.

Dahl himself informs us that leaders do not merely respond to the preferences of individuals, they also shape them (1961, p. 164). But we need not assume that this is always done by individuals acting intentionally. Take Dahl's observation that in the USA almost the entire adult population has been subject to some degree of indoctrination through the schools. This is reinforced in adult life through 'normal exposure to the democratic creed' (1961, p. 317). Although pressures like these involve an expression of power—some policy options are legitimated, others are not—it is clear from Dahl's own examples that this process of 'indoctrination' and 'exposure' is institutional and structural (rather than individual and intentional) in character. It is the consequence of a multitude of activities, none of which necessarily sets out with the intention of consciously excluding from consideration this or that social alternative.

But what is the result? The three-dimensional view of power begins to sound increasingly bizarre. A conflict which might have materialised, remains 'latent'; decisions which could have been taken fail to materialise; and issues which might have surfaced are suppressed. A non-event taken by no one in particular points positively nevertheless to a concentration of power in the hands of an elite! It is hardly surprising that when confronted with an argument like this, the behaviouralist defenders of pluralism are not usually impressed.

The three-dimensional view of power has a further implication which has also proved explosively controversial. To argue that nondecision-making and consensus works to suppress conflict suggests that compliant individuals may express preferences which are at variance with their real interests. It is to imply that were the processes of indoctrination and ideological exposure less effective or constraining, then these preferences would change and conflict would erupt.

Both the behavioural and the two-dimensional analysts of power find this implication politically suspect and philosophically unconvincing. Politically, the claim, it embraces a logic of authoritarianism since it appears to be asserting that the investigator can know what is in a person's *real* interests even when the people themselves do not. The distinction between real as opposed to professed interests raises the Rousseauan spectre of an authoritarian General Will forcing people to be free. Philosophically, it implies a 'non-empirical' view of human nature. People can have real interests even where they don't manifestly express them (Barry, 1975, p. 253). The three-dimensional view, it seems, broadens the concept of power to such a degree that it becomes morally obnoxious and methodologically untenable.

Lukes concedes that there is a problem. Whether conceived as the intentional act of an individual or as the sheer weight of institutional pressure, the exercise of power must always, he accepts, create a situation in which someone does something which they would not otherwise have done. A 'counter-factual' must be found which enables us to suppose that those ruled over would have acted differently were it not for the power of those ruling over them. But here is the rub. If there is merely 'latent' conflict, a potential event and a non-existent decision, nothing, it would seem, has actually taken place. How then do we identify the counter-factual which suggests that things could have been otherwise? The structures which have power and the agents who must nevertheless exercise it are spliced apart: an *act* of power becomes an analytical impossibility.

Lukes's response to this problem is most interesting. Drawing upon Matthew Crenson's study of air pollution as an issue in American cities, Lukes emphasises the point that even where nothing happens—no decisions are taken, no issues arise—this *inactivity* may still have manifest, tangible and wholly empirical consequences. Crenson's comparative study of East Chicago and Gary reveals that in one case, an ordinance regulating air pollution was passed in 1949, while in the other it was delayed until 1962. People were being poisoned in one city long after they had obtained a measure of pollution protection in another. That is one empirical fact. In Gary, a single steel company dominated the city and there was a strong party organisation; in East Chicago there were a number of steel companies and a weaker party organisation. That is another empirical fact.

These facts, when comparatively presented, provide the 'counter-factual' evidence that but for the indirect and potential influence of big business over local government, things could have been different. They point to the empirical existence of a non-issue (i.e. air pollution), and to the mechanism (i.e. politicians in awe of business's reputation of power) which kept this non-issue off the agenda. These facts make it possible, in other words, to suggest that there actually existed a latent conflict in the city of Gary for over ten years.

Hence the case study can also provide a solution to the thorny problem of preference vs. interest. Unless we assume (somewhat ludicrously) that people in Gary wished to be poisoned while those in East Chicago did not, it seems perfectly plausible to take the view that the people in Gary put up with a situation which was contrary to their real interests. (A possible fear that tackling pollution earlier would have created unemployment does not seem to have featured in this case.) In other words, had power been 'exercised' in a less monolithic manner, then the people of Gary would have changed their minds.

It is not necessary to argue that this power was being intentionally exercised by the steel company or that people were being intentionally poisoned. It is enough merely to observe that industrial enterprises are structured in a way that they are unsympathetic to policies which hinder the maximisation of short-term profits, and that politicians are wary of industry's potential power. The Crenson study demonstrates, therefore, that even where issues are suppressed through nondecision-making and consensus, the relevant counter-factual and the mechanism exercising this elite power can still be identified (1974, p. 45).

The exercise of power is not therefore simply a question of individual will. The unintended consequences of collective action cannot be discounted (Oppenheim, 1981, p. 46). Indeed, it might even be argued that what Lukes does in his 'radical analysis' is to tease out some of the methodological implications of *Who Governs?* since Dahl himself points to the indirect and potential influence of groups, and to the existence of institutional pressures which may quite unconsciously shape preferences. Lukes has, I think, shown convincingly that power can arise through collective structures as well as individual agents: that it is a product not merely of will, but of the natural and social circumstances which mould people's behaviour.

This question of structure is not only central to the three-dimensional view of power and its critique of the pluralists. It also offers a crucial insight into the authority-power relationship. For the dilemmas of the structural argument are precisely those which make the relationship between power and authority a contradictory one.

At the beginning of this section, we asked the question: how can force ever be 'legitimate'? How can individuals be moral agents, and yet at the same time be compelled by the state's concentrated power? Some have suggested that individuals in society can act freely in a way which seems unthinkable in the context of the state. But why should conceptualising power in a social realm make it possible to identify pure authority? If our 'two levels' are fused together in public, what makes them separable in private?

The dimensions debate suggests that this scepticism about a 'social' divorce for power and authority is well founded. Wherever there are social structures, institutions or collectivities, there is a problem. It is not merely the concentrated agencies of the state which constrain freedom and impose power; it is also the diffuse pressures of social structures. The problem then is this. Can we still be agents if at the same time our activity is structurally patterned? Can we be said to respect authority, i.e. autonomously comply with the requests of another, if at the same time we are moulded by the realities of power?

In other words, the contradictory relationship which troubles us in a political context remains problematic in a purely social one as well. Coercive pressures can arise simply through the weight of institutions and the patterning of social relationships. It is true that the dimensions debate does not specifically exclude the existence of the state. But the kind of institutional and collective pressures which surface in the three-dimensional view of power are not peculiar to societies with a state. They would also arise in a society without one, since it is difficult to imagine *any* society without structural influences of some kind or another. Indeed in our earlier discussion about stateless societies, we identified numerous forms of non-statist coercion employed to sustain social order.

Our problem therefore is not merely political—a problem of the concentrated power of the state. It raises thorny questions about the problem of individual autonomy and social determination in general: questions which lie at the root of the contradictory relationship between power and authority. Progress will be possible only if we know turn our attention to what might be called the philosophical aspects of the dimensions debate.

6 Taming the Centaur: Can the Riddle be Solved?

HOW DOES THE RULING CLASS RULE? A MARXIST DEBATE

Working our way through the dimensions debate has alerted us to the problem of structure and agency. Whereas the behaviouralists seek to analyse power in terms of individual will, their radical critics insist that the activity of individuals can be understood only in contexts which are structural in character.

In confronting the question of structure, we can register an important step forward in our conceptual analysis, for it is now possible to see that the paradoxical relationship between power and authority goes beyond the problem of the state. Its roots lie in the fact that people enjoy autonomy as agents in a world in which they are compelled to do things. True, this compulsion is concentrated in the state but it is also diffused throughout social institutions in general. Abstracting human relations from the state will not in itself solve our problem. It is from the structural character of society itself that our problem arises.

This emphasis on structure is one which the Marxist tradition finds particularly congenial. People make their own history but not in circumstances of their choosing. They enter into social relationships 'independent of their will'. As Ball has argued, two strikingly different concepts of coercion can be found in political theory. The classical liberal notion, which presupposes intention and postulates the exercise of power through an 'individuated' will; and the Marxist concept of coercion, which is 'relational' in character. Individuals play social roles in a collective drama written by no one and everyone: their individual wills are socially determined. For Marxists, therefore, coercion arises through structural relationships, whereas for liberals, it is the expression of an atomistic will.

It is not difficult to see the problem which this atomism poses. It implies that where repression is not explicitly intentional but merely structural, then it doesn't really count. On this argument, for example, the master-slave relationship cannot be deemed coercive because slaves are not independent individuals intentionally repressed by their masters! The coercion of slaves by their masters arises as the result of the social role which each plays in a system whose repression is structural in character; it cannot be explained in terms of a atomised world of individual wills (Ball, 1978, p. 100).

If, however, the atomistic or 'voluntaristic' view of power creates problems for liberals, the structuralistic view is not without its difficulties either, and this is a point which the Marxists themselves have had to acknowledge. By the late 1960s the dimensions debate (which had begun a decade earlier between liberals and radicals) now spilled over into a debate among Marxists as to how best to tackle the problem of structure and agency in capitalist societies. Confronted with the need to produce their own critique of pluralism, Marxists inevitably found themselves brought face to face with the dilemma which arise from the three-dimensional view of power.

It is one thing to insist that beyond the observable activity of decision-making there lies, as we have seen, the indirect and potential influence of the nondecision-makers—a world of institutions and structures which contrive to create a consensus and constrain the activists. But where do we go from here? How do we characterise the constraints which these collectivities impose? Can it be said that 'social causation', the social patterning engendered by institutions, is itself an activity? Where do we draw the line between structural determination and the *exercise* of power?

This is why it is that Lukes ends his 'radical analysis' of one debate by reviewing another: the debate between Nicos Poulantzas, a 'structuralist' influenced by the French Marxist

Louis Althusser, and Ralph Miliband, a political sociologist impressed by the power-elite analysis of C. Wright Mills. Both protagonists, as we shall now see, are Marxists sympathetic to a three-dimensional view of power, and both are conscious of the conceptual dilemmas which its structuralism raises.

In 1969 Miliband produced a major study of the 'Western system of power', *The State in Capitalist Society*, in which he placed a particular emphasis on the social background of the functionaries of the state—the army generals, judges, civil servants, cabinet ministers, etc. This social background, Miliband argued, is important because it provides the basis for that community of interest which exists between the world of business and finance on the one hand, and the state on the other. It is a basic fact of life that the vast majority of people in Western societies are governed, represented, judged and commanded in war by people who are drawn from economically and socially superior classes (1973, p. 62). Though fiercely critical of the pluralists, Miliband still considered it relevant to pose Dahl's famous question: who governs? Running the state is an *activity* central to any system of power. Hence it is crucial that we investigate the character of those who run it.

While Miliband was still writing *The State in Capitalist Society*, a very different kind of Marxist argument had just been constructed. In his *Political Power and Social Classes* (first published in 1968), Nicos Poulantzas insisted, in opposition to 'subjectivist' accounts of power, that the capitalist state cannot be understood as the instrument or the 'agent' of a dominant class. It exists rather as 'en ensemble of structures' which has the particular function of providing cohesion to capitalist society as a whole (1973a, p. 43; p. 288). What this state does is much more important than the people who do it. Shortly after completing his own structuralist classic, Poulantzas reviewed Miliband's book, and not surprisingly was highly critical.

The gist of his critique is this. Miliband, he argues, has made the mistake of assuming that people are 'social actors' within a system of power, so that the class character of this system can be analysed in terms of the 'inter-personal' relationships which exist between business and finance on the one hand, and state functionaries on the other. In other words, Miliband has failed to get to grips with the fact that social classes and the state constitute 'objective structures'. These structures constitute 'a system of regular connections' whose agents are merely the 'bearers' of objective relationships (1973b, p. 295). It follows from this argument that the social background of those who run the state is neither here nor there. If people from a bourgeois background also participate in the political system, that is not the cause but merely the effect of an 'objective relation'.

The fact is that the state functions to reproduce the conditions necessary for a capitalist society *whatever* the social background of those in charge. Indeed one can even argue, says Poulantzas, that the capitalist state best serves the interests of a capitalist class when the members of this class do *not* directly participate in running the state. Miliband, in a word, is barking up the wrong tree. His preoccupation with the background of those who govern flies in the face of Marx's own contention that individuals cannot be held personally responsible for their social relationships. His agency-oriented analysis suggests that, trapped in the 'problematic of the subject', he has not really understood the importance of structure.

In his reply to Poulantzas, Miliband concedes that the structural constraints which a system places upon the freedom of actors are important. Indeed it is noteworthy that in his later work on Marxist political theory Miliband gives these structural factors rather more emphasis than he does in *The State in Capitalist Society*. Nevertheless he is basically unmoved by the Poulantzas critique. Poulantzas, he argues, appears to place an exclusive stress on the capitalist state as a system of objective relations. As a result, the structural constraints of the system become to compelling that they threaten to turn those who run the state into the merest functionaries. Indeed, in what sense can it be said that, as the mere 'bearers' of the system, these functionaries run the state at all?

Poulantzas's analysis, in other words, overreaches itself. It collapses into a kind of structural determinism or 'super-determinism' which makes it impossible to consider realistically 'the dialectical relationship' between the state and capitalism (1970, p. 57). It blurs almost to the point of obliteration the linkage between the activity of functionaries and the structures which constrain them.

Poulantzas's analysis (Miliband might have pointed out) also makes the capitalist state appear all powerful and immune to the forces of change, since unless we can identify 'subjects' who act, how is one system to be transformed into another? It is surely ironic that a Marxist revolutionary (critical of the 'conservatism' of orthodox communists) should unwittingly conjure up the spectre of the 'equilibrium bias' which has haunted structural-functionalists since the 1950s. For if the system functions through objective structures alone, how can it change?

This question of determinism, structuralism and change takes us, as Lukes notes in his review of the Miliband-Poulantzas debate, to the heart of the matter. Can a person be said to exercise power unless he or she also has responsibility for their acts? We have to assume, when power is being exercised, that the person exercising this power could have acted differently—that had power not been exercised, things would have been *otherwise*. This problem emerges with particular poignancy in the 'post-Marxist' radicalism of Michel Foucault, when he argues that power is not something which individuals hold. Power is a force which creates its own human subjects as an impersonal machine divorced from human agency (Fine, 1984, pp. 192–3). Yet there must be more to power than simply 'structures'. Unless, as Lukes insists, we can locate the point at which structural determination ends and responsible activity begins, we hardly have a concept of power at all (1974, p. 56).

It would seem therefore that the Miliband-Poulantzas debate reinforces rather than resolves the problem of structure and agency raised by the dimensions debate. In particular, it prompts a rather intriguing question.

ARE THE MARXISTS HOIST ON THEIR OWN PETARD?

Our problem is this. The behavioural conception of power as 'observable' decision-making is superficial and one-sided.

Indeed Dahl himself feels compelled to move beyond it in practice, if not in theory. But the more we *broaden* our conception of power, the more structural it becomes. The more structural it becomes, the more difficult it is to speak of power as an activity (i.e. the more difficult it becomes to speak of power at all).

This problem is well exemplified by Marx (1976a, p. 329) in a joint work he wrote with Engels in 1845. Here he appears to endorse the position of theorists like Hobbes who, he says, have taken 'power' as 'the basis of right' (i.e. the state), as opposed to theorists who have taken 'will' as 'the basis of right'. This conceptual juxtaposition poses our problem very sharply indeed. For if power is something other than 'will', what can it be? How can people be said to exercise power unless this is, at the same time, a *willed* activity?

The bearing which this problem has upon the contradictory relationship between power and authority can be seen very clearly if we stay for a moment with Hobbes. The *Leviathan*, it should be remembered, appears to present a militantly deterministic view of the world by radically challenging the notion of a 'pure' or voluntaristic freedom. While it is true, Hobbes tells us, that actions proceed from liberty, it is also true that every act 'proceedeth from some cause, and that from another cause' (1968, p. 263). Freedom is the recognition of necessity. But if power here means causality, i.e. structural determination, what has become of authority? If people are always compelled by 'causes', where then is that element of autonomy, that moral responsibility which the very exercise of power itself presupposes? Hobbes denies that the power of the ruler over a subject is simply a kind of physical force like the 'power' of a stone to smash down a wall. The power he is concerned with is the power to be free; the capacity to do as one wills (1968, p. 262). But this seems to point the concept in two directions at the same time, since the inclination and desire to do as one wills appears to be the very opposite of power as (compulsive) causality.

Hobbes's argument is a remarkable one. You are free, he says, when you do what (a deist) God wills you to do. *Your* freedom stems from God's 'necessity', i.e. from the causal chains of the universe. What makes you free is the fact that while you act according to necessity, you do so from *choice*. Likewise with the problem of power and authority. It is possible for a commonwealth to be established by *conquest* because in this situation the vanquished recognise (as indeed they must) the right of the victor to rule over them. They are not slaves—mere physical bodies—but subjects who express in words or by 'other sufficient signes of the Will' that they wish to serve. It is not, Hobbes insists, the 'victory' as such that gives the right of dominion over the vanquished but the vanquished's own 'Covenant'. They are obliged not because they are conquered but because they 'submitteth to the Victor' (1968, p. 256). Force and fear are perfectly consistent with freedom and consent.

The state therefore is legitimate because all political power involves the right of the victor to rule over the vanquished. Power necessarily implies authority because people accept the constraints that institutions place upon them. Whether they accept these restraints out of fear or out of respect, because they are intimidated or because they are morally convinced matters not. Both power and authority 'proceedeth from necessity': you willingly do what has to be done. Power and authority appear to be one and the same.

It is hardly surprising that this is an argument which alarmed Hobbes's critics. Rousseau, for example, characterised it as a method of reasoning which offers 'fact as a proof of right'. It assumes that every structure of power is legitimate simply because people must in some minimal sense recognise its existence. 'It is possible to imagine a more logical method, but not one more favourable to tyrants' (1968, p. 51). As far as Rousseau is concerned, Hobbes treats humans as cattle. It is true that Hobbes insists (as we have just seen) that servants are not *slaves*: slaves have no obligation to obey, whereas servants have made a promise to their masters. But Rousseau is not impressed. Why not go the whole hog and argue with Aristotle that slaves (like servants) 'love their servitude' (1968, p. 52) and therefore recognise the right of their master to own them?

As Hannah Arendt reminded us earlier, the ownership of slaves itself can be sustained organisationally and socially only when there is some mutual recognition among the parties involved (1970, p. 50). If the vanquished can 'consent', why can't slaves? And once we accept that slaves also have to 'submitteth' to their masters, then it follows in terms of the Hobbesian argument, that slavery itself involves authority as well as power. Power is legitimate simply because it is *there*. The paradoxical relationship between power and authority is not resolved: it is merely conjured out of existence by a definitional sleight of hand.

Certainly Crick is clear that this is no way to defend politics. Where everything is knowable, determined or certain, freedom is impossible, and thus politics itself is extinguished. 'Free actions are always, strictly speaking, unnecessary actions' (1982, p. 54). Once we collapse authority into power and reduce power to mere causality, then anything seems possible. The language of necessity, says Crick tersely, spells the death of freedom and 'usually of men too' (1982, p. 106).

This leaves us with the following problem. Is it possible for Marxists to advance beyond the materialism of Hobbes without embracing the idealism of Rousseau? While Hobbes reduces authority to power in a way which appears morally suspect, Rousseau simply abstracts authority from power in a way which is logically mystifying. If, as Rousseau suggests, power and force can never be legitimate—'force is a physical power; I do not see how its effects could produce morality' (1968, p. 52)—how then we can make sense of the state? After all, it is not Rousseau's contention that all states are devoid of morality, but rather that political power must be based upon the 'will'. However, according to Rousseau, acts of will are 'purely spiritual and wholly inexplicable by the laws of mechanism' (1973, p. 54). Authority (it would seem) arises from within a mysterious world of its own. Thus, while Hobbes collapses freedom into necessity, Roussseau wrenches them apart.

But how is Marx to avoid the problems of both? As a determinist, Marx certainly sees freedom as governed by necessity. The view of power which he presents in *Capital*, for example, is a very three-dimensional affair. The advance of capitalist production develops, Marx argues, a working class which by education, tradition and habit looks upon capitalist conditions 'as self-evident laws of Nature'. Force expresses itself here not merely in the concentrated agencies of the state, but in what Marx calls the 'dull compulsion of economic relations which completes the subjection of the labourer to the capitalist' (1970, p. 737).

In other words, it is not merely the state which coerces. So do circumstances. This social coercion moreover not only extends to workers who are compelled to sell their labour power 'voluntarily' to capitalists. Capitalists are also coerced by the 'laws of competition'. Indeed, even when people confront one another not as workers and capitalist but as the independent producers of commodities, they still suffer what Marx describes as 'the coercion exerted by the presence of their mutual interests' (1970, p. 356). Macpherson might take Milton Friedman's point that (at least) in the 'simple market model' cooperation is achieved without coercion but Marx disagrees. There may be morality, authority, freedom, equal rights, mutual interests and (Marx adds) 'Jeremy Bentham' for good measure (1970, p. 176) in the world of perfect competition but there is still coercion!

The market mechanism itself involves relationships of coercion and power. But what about society in general? If Marx regards it as a *general* principle that people enter into social relationships 'independent of their will', then the whole of humankind appears subject to a tyranny of circumstances. Not only a world of power without authority but, as we have seen, a world in which the very idea of power as an activity becomes highly problematic.

It is true that this broad 'social' concept of coercion is not peculiar to Marx. We have already encountered it in our discussion on stateless societies, and it can be found, for example, in J.S. Mill's classic, *On Liberty*. But while Mill refers to social pressures (like those of public opinion) as despotic and coercive, he is concerned with escaping from them. It may well be argued that in this he is far from successful. But at least he tries. For Marx, on the other hand, all are inexorably subject to the coercion of circumstances. The determinism of his argument is explicit, forthright and foundational. People enter into relations independent of their will.

Yet Marx is acutely conscious nevertheless of the conceptual problems which determinism can bring. Past materialists, he complains, have failed to explain the importance of *activity*—the fact that circumstances not only change people, but that people change circumstances. The educator must be educated (1976a, p. 7).

In *Capital* Marx appears to deepen the dilemmas of his deterministic stance by insisting that human production is a purposive activity. Unlike bees, architects raise a structure in their imagination before erecting it in reality (1970, p. 178). On the one hand (Marx tells us), people enter into productive relationships independent of their will, and yet, on the other, he insists that this production is possible only as a willed activity. People, Marx seems to be saying, must be agents (otherwise they couldn't produce) but this agency can be identified only through the structures which constrain it! What is offered with the one hand is apparently taken away with the other.

Has not the 'pupil of the mighty Hegel' thoroughly tied himself up in knots? Marx does, I shall argue, have a way out of this problem. It is not one which theorists schooled in the liberal tradition are normally willing to accept but it is a plausible escape route nevertheless. What it involves, however, is not less determinism (than, say, the Hobbesian 'solution' to the question), but in fact rather *more*.

Marx's answer might be formulated thus. People are indeed the product of their circumstances (as the materialists assert) but it is important not be half-hearted about this proposition. People, it should be stressed, are *wholly* (and not just partially) the product of circumstances. It is not merely their 'physical' appetites which arise from the material world—it is their mental faculties as well. The individual produces and consumes as a 'whole' person (Marx and Engels, 1975, p. 299). Everything about us is determined; there is no purely autonomous realm of reason or spirituality which can be said to inhabit a world of its own.

Marx breaks, in other words, with the residual dualism of earlier materialists by rejecting the idea that human consciousness is some kind of ghost within the machine: the creation of God through nature. Hence he characterises the materialism of Hobbes and the Enlightenment as an 'abstract materialism' (Hoffman, 1984, pp. 116–17). It is an *abstract* materialism because it cannot account concretely for the human act. Unable to explain what it is that creates the creator, earlier materialism falls back upon deism as a result. Its determinism is thus partial and inconsistent.

This is why Marx and Engels are so enthusiastic about Darwin. Darwin, Marx tells us in *Capital*, throws important light on what might be called the 'genesis of genesis': the origins of human creativity. This is because his theory of evolution provides the basis for a 'history of the productive organs of man' (1970, p. 372). It is clear that by 'organs', Marx is referring here not just to human tools but to human *faculties*. Darwin has made it possible to analyse freedom in consistently deterministic terms, because his theory of evolution enables us to explain how humans, in the course of their protracted development from the animal world, come to acquire that mental and manual dexterity which enables them to produce. In other words, the fact that humans are a product of circumstances enables us to understand how they become the *producers* of circumstances. They can purposively modify their environment because of the peculiar way in which they have evolved from this environment. They are natural beings who have humanised themselves on an evolutionary timescale.

Two crucial points follow from this argument. The first is that there is no longer a need to invoke an external deist creator to explain the development of human spirituality and will-power, for this spiritual and physical creativity emerges through an evolutionary process of 'nature developing into man' (Marx and Engels, 1975, p. 304). The producers of circumstances are themselves the product of circumstances. Secondly, this evolutionary process transforms humans as a whole so that, as Marx puts it, all the human senses 'become directly in their practice *theoreticians*' (1975, p. 300). It is now possible to break completely with the old dualist view (shared by past materialists and idealists alike) that humans are beasts with red cheeks—contradictory amalgams of a spiritless flesh at war with a fleshless spirit.

Just as the dualism between spirit and nature dissolves, so too does the old juxtaposition between freedom and necessity. People are free because (a) they recognise necessity in order (b) to transform it. Both notions are entailed in a coherent view of human activity. Bluhm is wrong therefore to argue that the 'dialectical resolution of the duality of mind and body and of freedom and force' inevitably sacrifices freedom to necessity (1984, p. 171). The structures which constrain us are either (natural) structures which we influence, or (social) structures which we wholly create. Human freedom is thus perfectly real.

But why should the 'social structures' which we create continue to constrain us? The answer is a simple one. Since our *capacity* to produce is itself a product of necessity, the social structures through which we produce, must also be a product of necessity. It is true that there are two different 'necessities' involved. The one is natural, the other social. The one is rooted in our evolutionary origins as an animal obliged to produce in order to survive. The other arises from the structures we create in order to make this production possible. But if the two 'necessities' are different, they are also linked.

The one necessity encapsulates and concentrates the other. We produce because we have to: that is an evolutionary fact. But we also produce because we want to. Production is possible only because we create a system of social structures with a freedom and a sense of purpose which no other animal has. That is a social fact. If our activity as social beings transcends our evolution as natural beings, this social activity still constitutes a new kind of necessity because our very freedom to create is itself a product of the circumstances which have made us what we are. In other words, social structures are a 'socialised' necessity rooted in the wider natural-historical necessity from which humans have evolved, and with which we continuously interact as producers.

That is why, as far as Marx is concerned, even this socialised part of our heritage constitutes a structural set of relationships which people enter independent of their will. These relationships make up the celebrated 'basis' in his theory of historical materialism, and he distinguishes basis from 'super-structure' because we can never, at any given point in time, wholly understand (and thus control) the social structures which constrain us. Our consciousness is necessarily a partial one. Not only are these social structures infinitely complex in themselves since they embrace the whole of our human past. They also form part of what Hegel liked to call 'the substantial totality of things' (1956, p. 36)—that wider process of natural history which is infinite in its evolutionary gradations and changing forms. Unless we believe that humans have some kind of divine capacity to grasp this 'substantial totality' as a whole, then we must accept that we can master only a finite part of that social and natural necessity which continues to structure our existence.

On this account, therefore, agency is tied to structure but it has nevertheless a specific identity of its own. As with the state-society relationship explored in the previous section, the distinction between structure and agency, necessity and freedom can only be 'methodological' in character. No one can act 'outside' a structure, and no social structure can exist 'outside' human activity. Even natural structures are continuously modified by everything we do. We are forever changing the circumstances which make us what we are. If the 'will'. (in Rousseau's terminology) emerges from 'mechanism', it does so with properties which are peculiar to it. No other force in nature is conscious and purposeful; spiritually and physically creative.

At the same time this activity 'proceedeth from some cause': its very autonomy has to be explained in terms of the structures which it transcends. The world *develops*: it does not simply 'move'. Spirit, to recall our earlier concept, 'concentrates' matter just as the state concentrates society. The conscious will has its own identity. But as a 'superstructure' it cannot be grasped except in terms of the 'base' it concentrates.

Marxists, we conclude, can make a sustained and serious attempt to avoid the mystical idealism of Rousseau and the 'abstract' materialism of Hobbes. A determinism is possible which links freedom and necessity, structure and agency in a way which avoids simply dissolving one into the other. As Hoffman's *First Law of Philosophical Obscurantism* (yet again) reminds us, the two are different and yet they are also the same. Yet even if we take this point, how precisely does this argument help us in tackling the contradictory relationship embodied in Machiavelli's centaur?

RECONSTRUCTING THE RELATIONSHIP BETWEEN POWER AND AUTHORITY

In exploring some of the philsophical problems which spring from the dimensions debate, we have contended that freedom is rooted in necessity, and that agency arises from within structure. Any attempt, in other words, to sort out the problem of the 'two levels' must begin with the reality of *power*. But this proposition need not be quite as 'illiberal' (or sinister) as it sounds. Indeed we can find support for our argument in Mill's *On Liberty*.

In this classic work, Mill argues a powerful case for toleration and individual autonomy. Where individuals act in a way which does not harm the interests of others, they should be allowed to do as they please. Yet, as Mill rightly insists, toleration does not imply indifference. Everything which happens in society has its consequences. Everyone affects everyone else. It follows therefore that if we choose to exercise our freedom in unconventional ways, we expose ourselves to those 'natural penalties' which society inflicts upon all who incur its distaste or contempt (1974, p. 150).

These penalties are not, however, to be confused with explicit punishments. They arise in situations in which we cannot be said to damage the interests of others, however much we may irritate or offend them. Natural penalties are, in a word, a response to eccentricity rather than wickedness. They involve, for example, avoiding a person's company and making clear the displeasure which their behaviour provokes. As 'penalties', they are not, strictly speaking, 'punitive' but they can certainly be 'very severe', and Mill calls them 'natural' because they arise as 'the spontaneous consequences' of our own actions (1974, p. 144). They do not express the considered moral judgments of others. As natural penalties, they remind us that we live in a world of inter-penetrating social relationships in which everything we do affects (even if it does not actually 'harm') everyone else.

This notion of a 'natural penalty' is an extremely fruitful one. It points to the fact that even where people are not being punished as a consequence of their acts, they are subject nevertheless to social pressures which are all pervasive. These social pressures can be legitimately characterised as 'natural penalties' because they are at least implicitly coercive in character. *Implicitly* coercive, because, as Mill emphasises, there is no intention here to inflict pain. The suffering arises incidentally from the fact that when we disapprove of a person's activity (even though not harmed by it), we simply use the same liberty in regulating our affairs that we allow others to use in regulating theirs (1974, p. 146).

The concept of a 'natural penalty' captures admirably the idea of a 'coercion through circumstances'. The natural penalty acts as a form of natural 'power' because as a result of experiencing it, we do something which we otherwise would not have done. Either we change our own behaviour (having been helped by society to see the 'error' of our ways), or we become even more committed to heterodox ideas or acts in the hope that society will begin to change *its* norms as a result.

It is clear therefore that Mill's notion of a natural penalty takes us beyond the kind of social coercion which is explicitly penal in character but which does not invoke the state's monopoly of legitimate force. In the case of natural penalties, coercion arises simply from the fact that as members of a society we cannot avoid acting individually in a way which has social consequences. It is clear that for Mill, the existence of these natural penalties does not *negate* freedom. On the contrary, he rightly regards them as indispensable for our self-development: unlike punishments and moral judgments, natural penalties enable people to learn for themselves.

This is why our analysis of the contradictory relationship between power and authority must be premissed upon the fact that, as one writer has eloquently put it, 'in a variety of subtle and complex ways, forms, and degrees, elements of coercion pervade and influence the intertices and landscape of human encounters' (Cook, 1972, pp. 108–9). Analysis must begin, in other words, with the reality of power in all its various statist and social forms. It follows that authority can no more exist in an abstract world of its own than the human will can exist outside of historical necessity. Authority must be identified as a dimension which arises from *within* power and as part of power. But the dependence is also mutual. If authority cannot exist apart from power, then power (at least in its social form) cannot exist apart from authority. All power is relational in character, and as we explore the role of power within social relationships, its linkage with authority becomes very evident.

All social relationships involve power—pressures (whether diffuse or concentrated) which constrain all who enter a given relationship. It is through these pressures that we become conscious of structure; of being compelled, implicitly or explicitly, to do that which otherwise we would not have done. But where does authority enter the picture? If a given relationship is to be sustained, then these constraints must not only exist, they must also be recognised. Hence they must necessarily be expressed as a set of defining ideals or expectations—as norms which can be said to define (and thus constrain) a relationship only because the parties involved *accept* them.

Herein lies the inseparable unity of authority and power. Unless this constraining norm is accepted, then the relationship itself cannot continue. Without authority, there is no power. People must recognise and accept the constraints placed upon them. No recognition, no relationship. On the other hand, unless the constraints are effective, and do define expectations in one way rather than another, encounters lose their cohesion. Without constraints, relationships are impossible. Take away one side of the power/authority equation and the other crumbles. No constraint, no relationship; no relationship, no authority. But how does this argument move us beyond Hobbes? Is there not a danger that this analysis merely robs authority of its specific identity, and is thus 'a method of reasoning' favourable to tyrants?

Let me respond to this objection by taking two diametrically opposed examples. The first is one which we have already touched upon—the master/slave relationship; the second—at the opposite pole of the autonomy spectrum—the relationship between doctor and patient. In both cases, I want to suggest that authority arises from within and as part of power, but that in each case, neither concept is simply dissolved into the other. Each can be analysed in a way which preserves its own distinct identity.

Take the grim and somewhat bizarre example of the slave. It has to be conceded that on my argument, even slavery appears 'authoritative'. It is an undeniable fact that unless slaves (however reluctantly or under whatever duress) 'acknowledge' or accept their slavery, they will either die or escape. A relationship between themselves and their masters presupposes conscious recognition of some kind. But does this not collapse authority into power in typically Hobbesian fashion?

Not if we remember the mutual character of all relationships. As Rousseau comments, 'those who think themselves the masters of others are indeed greater slaves than they' (1968, p. 49). Masters not only constrain their slaves; slaves also constrain their masters, even if the one constraint creates pleasure and the other pain. Being a slave limits your freedom, but so too does *having* one (even if in one case the inconvenience is catastrophic and in the other it is highly advantageous). The point is that the force slave holders exercise is constrained by the nature of their role. To put the point *in extremis*. Slave owners who simply kill their slaves or fail to keep them in service destroy the basis of their own power. Even the slave, in other words, makes some input into this most repressive of relationships, and it is this 'input' which gives the relationship its (minimally) moral and authoritative character.

Of course, we would want to say that in this instance, slave owners exercise 'much' power and 'little' authority. We make this judgment because of the *kind* of coercion which predominates—a coercion which is likely to be explicit and highly concentrated. This is why it is difficult (if not impossible) to imagine the institution of slavery except in the context of state's monopoly of legitimate force. Slaves who are expected to obey their masters simply through natural penalties or through moral compulsion alone would almost certainly all escape!

But even in a relationship where the coercive power employed is brutally explicit and highly concentrated, it has to be said that the dimension of authority is not wholly subsumed into that of power. It still has an identity of its own. For contrary to classical liberal prejudice, slaves are not just things: they are human beings who form relationships, and they can do so only through some (albeit minimal) exercise of an autonomous will. The force of their oppressor has to be recognised if the relationship is to be sustained, and herein resides its (flimsy but real) legitimacy and authority. Moreover, in a highly inegalitarian way, the constraints of the relationship are mutual: masters and slaves change places. In both cases, it is the authoritative dimension of the relationship that compels each party to act in a defined and specific way. Norms have to be moral in order to be compulsory. They have to be recognised in order to be effective.

We turn now to a relationship at the other end of the autonomy spectrum, that between doctor and patient (or if this seems insufficiently 'idealised', we could choose the teacher/pupil, priest/parishioner relationship instead). Here force, as it is conventionally defined, is not involved. As we noted earlier, this relationship is taken by Carter, for example, to exemplify the case of authority without power. Clearly it can be said that under normal circumstances, no concentrated coercion is brought into play. Patients go to doctors because they want to, and if they accept the advice proffered, this is (again normally) because they receive a rational communication of a persuasive or potentially persuasive kind. Certainly authority predominates in this relationship but is it true to say that there is no power?

It is here that the 'coercion of circumstances' becomes conceptually crucial. Doctors communicate to patients through invoking a world of circumstantial coercion or natural penalties. If the advice which they offer is not taken, it is clear that highly undesirable consequences will follow! In these circumstances the patient may have as little or as much freedom to choose as in a situation where the coercion employed is of a brutal and concentrated kind, for what choice does a chronically ill person really have if the alternative to accepting medical advice, is a swift and certain death?

Of course, in this case, it is not the doctor who inflicts the punishment. But the consequences are scarcely less painful or coercive simply because they are 'natural' and unintended in character. The circumstances here are likely to compel even the most autonomous individual to change course. Indeed however sensitively doctors advise their patients, if their communications do not invoke a coercion of a circumstantial kind, they are hardly likely to be persuasive. Doctors who are unable to persuade their patients to do as they are told, cease to be doctors. Without the exercise of power of *some* kind, even the most authoritative of relationships simply disintegrates.

Here again our concept of concentration is helpful. Diffuse social power may involve a whole range of pressures—from the invocation of natural penalties which arise inevitably as the social consequences of an individual act, through to moral sanctions which intentionally punish even though the explicit force of the state is not involved. As the coercion employed becomes more concentrated, so the chastening force of circumstances is, so to speak, gathered up and concentrated into deliberate acts. Social pressures become transformed into laws backed by the institutionalised coercion of the state. As the process of concentration deepens, so the authoritative dimension of the relationship diminishes, and the exercise of power becomes increasingly 'naked' in character.

There is therefore a real point to distinguishing the two levels of the Machiavellian centaur. Being coerced through the unintended circumstances of nature and society is rather different to being subject to the concentrated coercion of the state. Other things being equal, the more authority which exists, the better. Self-discipline is more desirable than a discipline which is explicitly and externally imposed. The differentiations noted earlier are indeed, as Dahl says, 'differences which make a difference' (1976, p. 42). But what we can now do is not merely separate differences out. We can also bring them back together. We can link up analytically differentiated 'forms of influence' in a coherently synthetic way.

The legitimate force of the state ceases to be a mystifying absurdity when we remember that all relationships, even those of a purely social kind, involve both power and authority. The presence of power and force in even the most authoritative relationship ceases to a tragedy, for once we understand the structural character of human activity, it is easy to see the concept of pure authority as a voluntaristic mirage. In one sense, authority and power pull against one another. The more authority a person or institution has, the less (direct and explicit) coercion is involved. But in another sense, the two levels are always in harness. One without the other would negate our very capacity to form relationships.

We return to Dahl's detailed taxonomy of 'influence' (1976, pp. 45–9), which we encountered at the beginning of this section. For now we can see how it is possible to make analytical distinctions within a 'synthetic unity'—to assess the authority/power relationship in a way which facilitates rather than fractures conceptual coherence. Dahl, we recall, analyses power or influence along a spectrum which runs from 'trained control' through to physical force. The key to making sense of this spectrum is the *interpenetrating* character of the power/authority relationship, even in situations where the coercion or force employed is of a purely circumstantial character.

Dahl's concept of 'trained control' involves the internalisation of former influential acts, though not necessarily of a persuasive kind. Hence we may well wish to query its existence at the 'authority' end of the spectrum. His 'rational persuasion' is clearly more overtly authoritative in character since a person who is rationally persuaded expresses a willingness to comply with instructions in a critical way. But here we must be crystal-clear as to what this rational persuasion actually involves. As we saw in the doctor-patient relationship, persuasion is authoritative only because it is able to invoke sanctions, not sanctions of an explicitly punitive kind, it is true, but the sanctions of 'life itself'—the unintended circumstances which follow as a consequence of every social act.

When persuasion yields to 'inducements', the power holder now plays a direct part in reordering these 'natural' circumstances. Intentionally contrived benefits co-exist with natural penalties as the source of influence. With 'power', as Dahl defines it, natural circumstances are still more extensively 'reordered' so that the benefits offered now exist alongside penalties which have been concentrated into deliberate punishments. With 'coercion' proper, only the concentrated punishments remain. Sanctions are threatened without the mitigating alternative of an inducement. When we come to 'physical force' at the power end of the spectrum, we encounter a coercion so concentrated that it momentarily disrupts the relationship between the power holder and recipient. For this reason, it would be better to say, as Lively does (1976, p. 8), that it is the *threat* of physical force (which may require periodic enactment to remain credible) which is relevant to power rather than the exercise of physical force *per se*.

It follows therefore that on this analysis, the existence of coercion within political and social relationships ceases to pose what Dahl calls a 'tragic dilemma' or a 'poignant and troubling' problem. Even the most authoritative relationship, even the purest and most rational kind of persuasion, is necessarily rooted in natural penalties—in coercion of a circumstantial kind. Hence we can dissolve away all those mystifying dualisms and immaculate conceptions which have bedevilled the analysis of authority and power for so long.

PART THREE
DEMOCRACY AND LIBERALISM

7 Promiscuity and the Cloud of Humbug

WHY THE AMBIGUITY?

Democracy is without doubt the most contested and controversial concept in political theory. To recall the theme of the introduction, it is the concept which most obviously spans the divide between theory and practice, ideology and political analysis. It is the concept which is most difficult to abstract from the concrete political world. Claims by linguistic analysts or behavioural political scientists that political theory must be free from 'compromising' value judgments are most difficult to sustain when democracy is discussed, for who can really stand aloof from public contention when 'the rule of the people' is under debate? Those who would merely clarify 'terminological muddles' or test 'hypotheses' are brought face to face with their own practical bias. But why *should* democracy be the most contentious of our contestable triad?

We encounter the first of many ironies. What makes democracy the most fiercely controversial of our three political concepts is the fact that, as a general principle, everyone (or almost everyone) appears to agree with it! Virtually every political stance in today's world invokes democracy as its hallowed *grundnorm*. 'All states today', as John Dunn comments criply, 'profess to be democracies because a democracy is what it is virtuous for a state to be' (1979, p. 11). If democracy enjoys a near universal acclaim as a conceptual shrine to which all seeking political virtue feel obliged to pay homage (or at least lip service), this is in part because it embodies such a wide range of contradictory meanings.

Socialists, liberals and conservatives; reactionaries and revolutionaries—all claim its allegiance. Majority rule and individual rights; limited government and popular sovereignty: private property and social ownership. Positions in the most manifest tension with one another are all defended in terms of the same concept. Representation vs. participation; the collective vs. the individual; socialism vs. capitalism. All are blessed in the name of democracy! As the conceptual battle commmences, each side emblazons its banners with the identical slogan.

No wonder many are confused. Some are even tempted to give up in despair (see, for example, the comments in the entry under 'Democracy' in the *International Encyclopedia of the Social Sciences*, 1968). Indeed Crick even goes so far as to demand that politics should be defended *against* democracy, not because he is opposed to democracy (at least not under all circumstances), but because he is in favour of clarity and precision as against vagueness and ambiguity. Democracy, he complains, is perhaps 'the most promiscuous word in the world of public affairs' (1982, p. 56).

Bernard Shaw devoted an entire play to the problem. His *Apple Cart* tackled the treacherous ambiguities of democracy with such flair that the play was actually banned by a nervous Weimar Republic, and in a witty preface to the work, Shaw complains that democracy seems to be everywhere and nowhere. It is a long word which we are expected to accept reverently without asking any searching questions. It seems quite impossible, Shaw protested, for politicians to make speeches about democracy or for journalists to report them without obscuring the concept 'in a cloud of humbug' (1930, p. xiv).

Hypocrisy, cant and humbug. The ambiguities of democracy inevitably remind us of Shakespeare's view of money as the 'visible God' that speak'st with every tongue to every purpose, or of Carl Becker's waspish description of democracy as a 'Gladstone bag'—the concept which can be made to accommodate (with a little manipulation) almost any collection of social facts (Hoffman, 1983, pp. 37–8). But why the tantalising and frustrating ambiguity of this concept above all others?

It is worth making the point that democracy has not always enjoyed a near universal acclaim. In the seventeenth century, for example, nobody who was anybody would have dreamt of calling themselves a *democract*. As far as people of 'substance' were concerned—landowners, merchants, lawyers and clergymen—democracy was a term of abuse. Not a good thing as Macpherson recalls, but a bad thing. A system of government fatal to individual freedom and to all the graces of civilised living (1966, p. 1). D.D. Raphael is startled to discover that even in the nineteenth century, socially minded liberals like J.S. Mill felt it necessary to defend liberty *against* democracy (1976, p. 143).

We have to wait, however, until after the First World War before democracy acquires its characteristic ambiguity, its Janus-faced capacity to point in all political directions at the same time. Even here acclaim has been uneven, and both right and left have sometimes vacillated. Hitler, for example, condemned democracy as the political analogue of economic communism, and declared that National Socialism is what Marxism could have been had it freed itself 'from the absurd, artificial link with the democractic system' (Dunn, 1979, p. 21). On the other hand, Mussolini found the hypocrisy of it all too tempting. In 1936 he announced in Berlin that 'the greatest and most genuine democracies which the world knows today are the German and the Italian' (Hoffman, 1983, p. 52)!

As far as the left is concerned, democracy has occasionally appeared irretrievably bourgeois or, as Trotsky once called it, 'counter-revolutionary' in character (Hoffman, 1984, p. 157). Arthur Rosenberg discovered a Communist Party secretary in Hamburg in 1923 who would rather burn in 'the fire of revolution than perish on the dung-heap of democracy' (1939, p. 9). But these somewhat 'leftist' formulations are rather atypical of the Marxist tradition which generally asserts the importance of democracy as part of the struggle for socialism.

Shaw's own solution to the cloud of humbug seems to have been a curious blend of both leftist and rightist vacillations. Can anyone, he speculates in the preface to *The Apple Cart*, really blame Mussolini for describing democracy 'as a putrefying corpse' (1930, p. xxiii)? We may all grumble about vagueness and ambiguity but this is an iconoclasm leaves most of us feeling distinctly uneasy.

It has to be said then that by the twentieth century, attacks on the concept of democracy have become the exception rather than the rule. Hence our basic problem. As long as democracy is condemned as a 'bad thing', it is at least possible to contrast vice with virtue, popular rule with autocracy. Once praise for democracy becomes wellnigh obligatory for politicians of almost every hue, so Gladstone bags and clouds of humbug reach mystifying proportions. Democracy becomes a bland synonym for 'All Things Bright and Beautiful' (Crick, 1956, p. 56), a hurrah word without any specific content. But why should a problem like this arise? If it was possible for theorists earlier to state bluntly their disagreement with democracy, why should the concept now appear in danger of dissolving into a miasma of hypocrisy and confusion?

Because democracy suffers from this tantalising ambiguity, it is a concept whose threads cannot be disentangled without historical analysis. It is only as we follow the twist and turns of its conceptual development that we can begin to acquire the perspective and contextual feel necessary to focus analysis. To grasp democracy, the conceptual and the historical must converge. Without a conceptual history of shifting senses and altered meanings, Gladstone bags and clouds of humbug will surely overwhelm us. Hence we shall need to dig deep into the past in this section in order to keep a grip on this most elusive of concepts.

Before we explore its tangled roots in the Old World, it is useful to look at democracy in the New, for it has been said that to explore democracy in the USA is to examine the concept under laboratory conditions, to locate it in its 'classic' surroundings. Even if this will not in itself make it possible to resolve all democracy's ambiguities, as we shall see, it will at least enable us to find a suitable partner for this most troublesome of theoretical constructs. In this way we can follow the practice adopted with the two other concepts analysed so far in this book.

DEMOCRACY AND THE AMERICAN POLITICAL TRADITION

We begin our conceptual historical analysis of democracy with an examination of its development in the American political tradition. This exercise will help us find a partner whose relationship to democracy makes it possible for us to begin to resolve the ambiguities· and absurdities of this difficult concept.

The words of Alexis de Tocqueville in 1835 have often been quoted: 'I saw in America more than America; it was the shape of democracy itself which I sought, its inclinations, character, prejudices and passions' (1966, p. 17). J.S. Mill was to describe *Democracy in America* as the first philosophical book ever written on the subject (1976, p. 188), and in it Tocqueville argues that only in the USA has the principle of popular sovereignty really been put into practice in a direct, unlimited and absolute way. Since Tocqueville, this assertion has come to enjoy the status of a revealed truth. We may argue about the Peoples' Democracies of Eastern Europe after the Second World War, Russia after 1917 or indeed the position of Britain at the turn of the century, but who would be brave enough to challenge the status of the USA as the 'most uncontested example' (Crick, 1982, p. 67) of a modern democracy?

It is therefore of interest to note that the American constitution was formulated in 1787 by people who were more than a little reluctant to identify themselves as democrats. Throughout the secret discussions at the Constitutional Convention, great distrust was expressed towards 'the common man and democratic rule': the struggles which had ensued in the eleven years since the Declaration of Independence appeared to many to exemplify 'the turbulence and follies of democracy' (Hofstadter, 1967, p. 4). Madison in the famous tenth Federalist Paper warned that democracies have ever been found 'incompatible with personal security or the rights of property'. Under a democracy, he argued, an egalitarian factionalism is likely to generate a rage for a paper money,for an abolition of debts or for some other 'improper or wicked project' (Hamilton *et al*, 1961, p. 81; p. 84). 'The people who own the country should govern it', John Jay declared, (Arblaster, 1984, p. 197), and all the Federalists endorsed the view that popular government becomes extremely dangerous when measures are decided by a strong and 'overbearing' majority. These reservations are not difficult to understand when we remember that the American Founding Fathers regarded themselves as republicans rather than democrats.

All this,however, raises an important question. If the constitution (which has remained essentially unchanged for over 200 years) was founded by people who were, to put it mildly, unenthusiastic about popular rule, why should Tocqueville and his admirers have regarded America as the classic home of democracy?

It might be argued that the Founding Fathers were conservative Federalists who lost influence to the more radical 'Democrats' who came to dominate the political scene after 1800—that most Americans identified less with Madison than with Jefferson, a man whom Tocqueville describes as 'the greatest democrat ever to spring from American democracy' (1966, p. 249). But this still does not wholly solve our problem.

After all, Jefferson himself not only admired the Federalist Papers but he shared to the full what one writer has called 'America's neurotic terror of the majority' (Hartz, 1955, p. 130). His democratic credentials are hardly above dispute. He favoured constitutional checks and balances as a way of preventing what he called 'elective despotism'. He was not enthusiastic about male universal suffrage, and he took the view that a democracy is desirable only when every citizen is a farmer who owns property! Even Jefferson, in other words, whose very name seems synonymous with democracy itself, was really a liberal in his political thinking.

Modern American folklore, as Hofstader (1967, p. 10) notes, has come to assume that 'liberty' (i.e. liberalism) and democracy are identical, and in this assumption we make our first breakthrough in tackling our problem of ambiguity. For the American political tradition reveals that if there is an 'intimacy almost inextricable' between liberalism and democracy, there is also, as Crick puts it, 'tension as well as harmony' (1982, p. 59). In fact, it is because there is both tension *and* harmony between the two that democracy has become such a slippery and elusive concept. Democracy's ambiguities are severely exacerbated by its relationship with liberalism. It is this tension and harmony, therefore, which we need to explore in depth if we are to have any success in penetrating the clouds of humbug and Gladstone bags already encountered.

The first problem focused by the relationship is this. The Founding Fathers may have thought of themselves as liberals and republicans, but the fact is that although they were not enthusiastic about democracy, they were not wholly opposed to the idea either. True, they feared that the poor would plunder the rich, but they were also conscious of the danger that without *some* popular restraint, the rich might plunder the poor. George Mason told the Philadelphia Convention that while 'we had been too democratic', he was afraid that 'we should incautiously run into the opposite extreme'. The people, it was agreed, must have a voice in making the laws, since, as John Adams put it, there can be 'no free government without a democratical branch in the constitution'(Hofstadter, 1967, p. 6; p. 14).

This then is the point. Democracy was to be *one* and only one element within a mixed or balanced constitution designed to ensure that the interests and right 'of every class' should be represented in the machinery of government. But if, as the Fathers also believed, democracies have ever been found incompatible with the rights of property, how was a compromise solution of this kind to be viable?

We come face to face with the secret of 'Democracy in America'. The Founding Fathers were liberals rather than democrats in a society in which there was an uniquely wide spread of property ownership. If American liberals were willing to contemplate a popular *element* in their constitution, this was because even the 'poor' themselves owned property, and hence could be more or less relied upon to act as responsible citizens with a stake in society. This is a point to which Tocqueville returns over and over again. Most people who are rich begin by being poor: there is greater equality of wealth and 'in mental endowments' in the USA than in any other country in the world or in any age of recorded history (1966, pp. 65–6). Moreover it is not just that the 'poor' of America might seem rich when compared to the poor of Europe (p. 258). They own their wealth as individual landowners.

America is democratic because there are no proletarians, although, it should be noted (and this is a point to which we will later return), there *were* dispossessed Indians and enslaved blacks whose plunder and exploitation is hardly incidental to explaining the ownership of property by most of the whites. As far as Tocqueville is concerned, the secret to America's success as a democracy is that 'everyone' has property to defend. Hence the extraordinary paradox. America is the land of democracy *par excellence*, and yet in no other country in the world is there a great love of property. Maxims called democratic in France would be outlawed in the United States (1966, p. 294; p. 828).

Tocqueville's analysis of the 1830s captures well the liberal egalitarianism of what has often been called 'Jacksonian democracy': a democracy based upon a sense of common identity derived from fighting the Indians, enslaving the blacks and owning land. Hofstadter describes it as the 'philosophy of a rising middle class' (1967, p. 61), and it was basically this philosophy which informed Lincoln's ideas as well. Lincoln attacked slavery, not because he was opposed to racism but because he feared that the spread of slavery would undermine the status of free white labour. And what made labour free? The fact that the hired labourer of today can hire labour tomorrow. If this position is egalitarian, the equality it champions is the equality of property owners in what is still basically a pre-industrial age.

Yet it was clear to Tocqueville that this equality had a curiously illusory dimension to it. For one thing, he notes, democratic institutions arouse a passion for equality which they are not really able to satisfy. Just as people think they have this equality in their grasp, it slips elusively through their fingers (1966, p. 245; also p. 695). And even more serious is the 'natural impulse', as Tocqueville calls it, which is 'throwing up an aristocracy out of the bosom of democracy'. In a chapter almost Marxian in tone, Tocqueville argues that as conditions become more equal, the need for manufactured products extends. The very rich open establishments with a strict division of labour, and the effect of this division of labour is to make workers degraded and dependent. The employer becomes more and more 'like the administrator of a huge empire' and the worker 'more like a brute'. 'Each occupies a place made for him, from which he does not move' (1966, p. 719). Clearly a development which causes anxiety for the 'friend of democracy', and yet Tocqueville takes comfort from two factors.

The first is that the development of a manufacturing aristocracy flourishes only in some industrial callings. It is an 'exception, a monstrosity, within the general social condition' (1966, p. 720). In other 'callings' market forces still reinforce the trend to greater equality. It is true, Tocqueville notes, that the effect of the great industrial undertakings is to depress wages so that workers are trapped in a vicious circle from which they cannot escape. But again he characterises this as a 'great and unfortunate exception' to the general trend within a democracy for equal conditions and rising wages to reinforce one another (1966, p. 754).

Tocqueville's second crumb of comfort arises from his belief that while the manufacturing aristocracy is 'one of the hardest that has ever appeared on earth', it is also one of the 'most restrained and least dangerous'. While the poor are becoming a class of oppressed proletarians, the rich lack the cohesion, corporate spirit and community of interest to become a class which rules (1966, pp. 720–1). They are, it would seem, too busy competing among themselves to exercise any collective control over the state.

Yet it is clear that on both these arguments, Tocqueville is vulnerable. In his review of *Democracy in America*, J.S. Mill wondered just how 'exceptional' manufacturing aristocracies were likely to remain in the USA. The British experience suggests that in all industrial and commercial 'callings', prosperity brings less rather than more equality. Great fortunes are continually accumulated but seldom distributed (1976, p. 237).

Mill's point was a salient one. The US census of 1870 showed that the trading classes were growing far more quickly than the population as a whole. By 1873 America had experienced its first serious industrial depression: a development spawning bankruptcies; mergers; wage cutting; urban riots; nation-wide strikes, and the use of troops by 'business-minded governments'. With industrialisation helping to speed up the concentration of wealth and power, 'the New World was beginning', as E.F. Goldman puts it, 'to repeat the Old World's dismal story' (1955, p. 5; pp. 26–7).

The Gilded Age, the Age of the Robber Barons, had arrived.

It was becoming clear, as the reform movements of the day protested, that the rich were making an impact upon the political process in precisely the way Tocqueville had discounted. Bribing Congressmen and buying legislatures were seen as an integral part of the capitalist ethic. The Senate became so full of business magnates that it was properly called the 'Millionaires Club'(Hofstadter, 1967, p. 166), and reformers targetted their energies on what one of them described as 'the alliance between industrialists and the political class which thinks like the industrialists' (Goldman, pp. 16–17). Manufacturing aristocrats, for all their internal competition, were coalescing into a new ruling class.

But what did this mean for democracy? Inevitably the industrial revolution, coming as it did in the wake of civil war, raised the problem of continuity with the past. Symbolising the optimism and expansiveness of the new era was Andrew Carnegie's *Triumphant Capitalism*, and what is significant about Carnegie's book is that it inaugurated a new conception of democracy in America. Democracy, as we have seen, had traditionally been identified with the popular element of the constitution. It was at best one element—an element to be checked and balanced by others. With *Triumphant Capitalism*, however, democracy now stood for the American system as a 'whole', and this at the very time when the egalitarianism upon which Tocqueville had laid so much stress was being called into question (Crick, 1959, p. 39; 1982, p. 68).

Carnegie's thesis found its resonances elsewhere. Whereas Bryce had merely noted that there was a 'strong plutocratic element infused into American democracy' (1889, p. 492), Sumner took the view that plutocracy *is* democracy in its truest form! 'The alchemy is complete' (McCloskey, 1967, p. 192). The slogans of the past have great political utility if they are 'carefully redefined'. Anyone who challenges the power of the manufacturing aristocrats must be anti-democratic, for true democracy is the system which preserves the fiction that the village stoorkeeper and the Standard Oil Company enter the economic arena on equal terms (McCloskey, 1967, pp. 189–95). In what has been described as 'one of the strangest reversals in the history of political thought' (Dahl, 1985, p. 82), democracy is transformed into liberalism, even (or even perhaps especially) in its least egalitarian form.

The scene is now set for the ambiguities of the twentieth century. It is true that under the impact of the First World War, pressures for a *rapprochment* between liberalism and democracy become evident in other countries as well. In Britain, for example, no one would have used the term democracy to describe the government in 1913 (Crick, 1982, p. 67), Yet just one year later, a war is fought to *preserve* this notable, if now somewhat flexible, political ideal! In the USA the effect of the war, as Woodrow Wilson himself had feared, is to strengthen the confidence of the right: conservatives do not merely demand the extirpation of the Bolshevik menace but they do so in the name of political democracy (Goldman, 1955, p. 211).

Yet despite the new found harmony, the tensions of the past still periodically reappear. A US Government publication in the 1920s defines democracy as 'a government of the masses ... Attitude towards property is communistic—negating property rights ... Results in demagogism, license, agitation, discontent, anarchy' (Goldman, 1955, p. 222). But such conceptual brutality has become exceptional, especially in the United States. What emerges, particularly in the period after the Second World War, is a compehensive reworking of the concept of democracy so that the ambiguities and alchemies gathering apace in the last years of the nineteenth century, now receive sustained, systematic and sophisticated elaboration.

While a veritable doyen of the American political science profession, Harold Lasswell, could draw upon the elite analysis of Pareto before the war in order to express an open scepticism towards the merits of popular rule, by 1942 he has become convinced that the most pressing task facing political scientists is the construction of a scientific theory of democracy. Politics is still defined in terms of elites but now he argues (in *Power and Personality*, 1948, for example) that the elite in a democracy includes everybody: the '"ruling class" is society-wide'. Whereas previously the USA (like all societies) had been ruled by the few, now happily it is ruled by the many, and as Easton points out (1950, p. 474), this remarkable transformation has been brought about without any tangible transfer of power having taken place!

Nor is Easton himself unaffected by conceptual alchemies which painlessly reconcile democracy to an inegalitarian status quo. In 1949 he declares that liberals are 'haunted' by the problem of the unaccountable power of wealth within the free enterprise economy. Just one year later these 'vast accumulations of wealth and power' (1949, p. 117; p. 37) disappear without trace. They are replaced by a much more 'relevant' question. Can the social scientist say whether 'the goals of a democratic society are superior to those of dictatorial communism?' (1950, p. 450). Democracy has ceased to be an ideal to be realised. It is a system which already exists, and the problem is how to defend it!

There can be little doubt that the anti-communism of the Cold War period accelerated this process of redefining democracy. President Truman told the American Political Science Association in 1947 that they had a singular responsibility to give the citizen 'a mature understanding' of the essentials of democratic government (Hoffman, 1983, p. 44), and, as the critical literature of the 1950s and 1960s pointed out, this 'democratic government' referred to the good society in operation: liberal societies as they were (inequalities and all) and not democratic societies as they might be.

In converting a critical concept into an apparently descriptive one, democracy had become, as Arblaster points out (1984, pp. 329–30), 'a conservative political idea'. Objections which conservatives and conservative liberals had levelled *against* democracy in the nineteenth century are now regarded as the identifying attributes of democracy itself. An unequal distribution of wealth; low level of popular participation; rule by elites (albeit with competition among themselves)—features which one contradicted the existence of democracy are now of its very essence.

This astonishing volte face is admirably exemplified by a comment in 1962 by Sartori (an Italian writer steeped in American political science). Democracy, he tells us, 'is so difficult that only expert and accountable elites can save it from the excesses of perfectionism, the vortex of demagogy' (Bachrach, 1967, p. 40). 'Perfectionism' and 'demagogy'—what had once sustained democracy (at least in the eyes of its conservative critics) now negates it. Democracy as redefined by Cold War liberalism has become the very antithesis of democracy as conceived by liberals in the past. Little wonder that so many were to be puzzled and perplexed by the democratic theorising of the post-war period.

What this brief excursion into the American political tradition has sought to highlight is the fact that behind these ambiguities lies the troubled relationship between liberalism and democracy. Louis Hartz has called America 'a triumph for the liberal idea' (1955, p. 17). Is it merely a coincidence that at the same time it is also the country whose political culture (both 'academic' and 'popular') emphasises, in a way more tantalising than in any other, the ambiguities of the democratic concept?

HYPOCRISY AND DECEPTION: DIGGING FOR THE ROOTS

The wellnigh universal acclaim accorded to democracy in the post-war period has certainly helped to generate clouds of humbug. In our argument up until now we have looked at this problem of mystification in the context of the changing relationship between liberalism and democracy. When liberals disapproved of democracy, its content was relatively precise: democracy was tied to popular participation and equality. But when liberals begin to applaud democracy (and the more unequal the distribution of power, the more vigorously they seem to applaud it), the term loses its precise meaning.

Yet, if this process of redefinition helps to account for the mystifying ambiguities of the democratic concept, it is not the whole story. True, the 'reduction' of democracy to liberalism involves elements of propaganda—ideological sleights of hand which make democracy serviceable as a stick with which to beat the communists. But what makes this redefinition possible and (for many) plausible in the first place? If the relationship between democracy and liberalism exacerbates our problems, we cannot hold the liberals *entirely* responsible for all the alchemies and ambiguities which we need to tackle.

We must now take our argument a step further. For in order to understand why the ambiguities of the concept of democracy are exacerbated by liberalism, we need to probe the character of popular rule before liberalism. The classical liberals in distancing themselves from democracy had taken their stance from an analysis of Greek antiquity.

The American Founding Fathers, for example, viewed with 'sensations of disgust and horror' what Madison called 'the turbulent democracies of ancient Greece', and they followed the Greek view that democracy was a system of government in which the people ruled directly (Hamilton *et al.*, 1961, p. 71; p. 100). Ancient definitions seemed painfully clear. Rousseau followed them when he defined democracy as 'a very small state' with a large measure of equality in 'social rank and fortune'. Yet is it true, as Rousseau and the other liberal critics of democracy robustly asserted, that this was a form of government ever liable 'to civil war and internecine strife' (1968, p. 113)?

By Greek democracy commentators generally mean the system of government which prevailed in Athens during the fourth and fifth centuries BC, and there is good reason to suppose that this ancient form of popular rule has been somewhat caricatured by its conservative and liberal critics. Greek democrats saw themselves as practical politicians and did not write treatises on the subject. Understandably, though unfortunately perhaps, they left the task of analysis to unsympathetic philosphers like Plato and Aristotle who saw in (particularly the 'extreme' forms of) democracy, the rule of demagogues and a chaotic moral 'anarchy' (for example, Aristotle, 1962, p. 244). Yet despite these disparaging commentaries, there is much to suggest that Athenian democracy was quite remarkable in character.

By 430 BC Athens was ruled by a popular assembly which met at least forty times a year. All citizens were not only allowed to attend the assembly but they were actually paid to do so. Each had the right to be heard in debate before decisions were taken, and the assembly had supreme powers of war, peace, making treaties and creating public works: in short, 'the whole gamut of governmental activity' (Finley, 1973, p. 19). Jurors, administrators and members of the 500-strong executive council were chosen by lot, and held office for only one or two years so that as a result, a considerable portion of male Athenian citizens had an experience of government 'almost beyond anything we can imagine' (Finley, 1973, p. 20; see also Dunn, 1979, pp. 16–17). Conservatives might paint lurid portraits of demagogues and crowd stirrers but it is a fact, says Finley, that except for two incidents during the Peloponnesian War, Athens was free from civil strife for nearly two centuries (1973, p. 48).

Sympathetic commentators have found it tempting to speak to Athenian democracy as 'pure' and 'genuine'—a democracy in which the ideal of popular rule flourished illustriously as a living reality. We have dwelt upon the Athenian experience because it might be supposed that in contrast to the inegalitarian plutocracies of the nineteenth and twentieth centuries, Greek democrats practised what they preached. At last a form of democracy free from all hypocritical humbug and tantalising ambiguity! Yet, of course, popular rule in Greece was rooted in slavery. Most employees in the mines and factories, in the police and on the farms were slaves. Engels calculates that at the height of its prosperity, there at least eighteen slaves to every male adult citizen in Athens (1972, p. 181) although others (Barker, 1959, p. 463; Held, 1987, p. 23) refer to a figure which is lower than this. In addition, women, like slaves, were excluded from public life, and resident aliens also had no political rights. The Athenian 'people' were really what one writer has called 'an exceptionally large and diversified ruling class' (Childe, 1964, p. 216).

If democracy was a government by the poor, the poor were still a minority of citizens. If they did not own slaves themselves, they certainly benefitted from slavery, and naturally enough they raised no objection to their relatively privileged status. Moreoever Athens was not only a slave society, but as Finley (1973, pp. 48–9) has rightly stressed, it was also an imperialist one. The payment for jury service, public office and membership of the executive council; the land settlement programme and the extensive distribution of public funds would not have been possible without the Athenian empire. Although he does not actually mention the importance of imperialism as such, Held notes that military successes brought 'material benefit to nearly all strata of Athenian citizenry'. (1987, p. 28). Democracy for some meant the subjugation and enslavement of others.

But what, one may ask, is problematic or ambiguous about that? After all, the Greeks were not liberals who claimed that all human beings are entitled to inalienable political rights. On the contrary, they made it perfectly clear that some are, as Aristotle put it, 'slaves by nature' (1962, p. 34). Rousseau might protest bitterly about this phrase, but he too acknowledges candidly that without slavery, Greek democracy would not have been possible (1968, p. 52; p. 142). Doubtless this is why virtually no Greek writer ever complained about slavery as an institution.

Yet ambiguity there still was, and this ambiguity is evident not only in the positions taken by conservatives. It is also evident in the positions taken by democrats. Conservatives like Aristotle feared that although Greek democracies functioned through the 'natural' hierarchy of citizen and slave, they had a tendency nevertheless to undermine the willingness of women, children and slaves to obey their respective masters (1962, p. 244).

Plato made the same point even more flamboyantly. Under a democracy he declares, natural hierarchies are turned upside down. Fathers and sons 'change places', and 'there's no distinction between citizens and alien and foreigner'. Slaves come to enjoy the same freedom as their owners 'not to mention the complete equality and liberty in the relations between the sexes generally'. In such a society 'the principle of liberty is bound to go to extremes', and in the end even the domestic animals are infected with anarchy (1955, p. 336)!

All this is surely intended as a hostile *reductio ad absurdum*, and it is hard to believe that Plato really thought that democrats in the ancient world would entertain libertarianism of this kind. But that is not the point. Plato's argument is a logical one. If people equate democracy with freedom and equality, why stop with adult male citizens? The principle of liberty is bound to go extremes. As a principle, it implies a potential universality which limited applications of the principle contradict. Herein lies its ambiguous character.

Of course, a Greek democrat could respond to Plato's attack by insisting that it wilfully confuses democracy as a form of the *state* with democracy as some kind of nebulous social principle. Greek democrats, it might be argued, were perfectly clear that democracy is a form of popular government that operates through the 'natural' hierarchies of the state, slavery, national and gender domination. They were clear, in other words, that democracy is a *political* rather than a social question. But were they?

Greeks lived to hark back to their 'ancestral constitution', and democrats, Barker tells us (1959, p. 449), sought to find in the prehistoric Theseus, the author and inventor of democracy. Certainly, it can be argued, that in the old clan system of tribal Greece the people ruled themselves. Here, declares an admiring Friedrich Engels, 'primitive democracy was still in its full strength' (1972, p. 167), and it is therefore understandable that democrats should look back to the past for inspiration. Greek constitutional history is revealing on this score. When Kleisthenes overthrew the oligarchs and forged a new constitution towards the end of the fifth century BC, the external features of the old tribal system were faithfully reproduced in the arrangements of the new. The popular assembly, the festivals, the use of the lot: all this made it appear that the people were simply recovering the ancient rights of their old tribal constitution.

The continuity, however, was deceptive. As Thomson comments, 'the democrats had triumphed; their hopes had been fulfilled; yet the result was the opposite of what they had intended' (1955, p. 227; see also Cone, 1986, p. 73). The clan system, which had once formed the basis for a 'primitive' democracy, had become by Kleisthenes's time a device for excluding commoners from political life. The new units of the constitution, though tribal in form, were really geographical in character. This made it possible for the reformers to introduce unobtrusively the revolutionary features of the new system so that first the disenfranchised middle classes, and then the citizenry as a whole, could exercise state power.

The irony is complete. The new democratic constitution which appeared to resemble the old so closely, actually worked to accelerate the final disintegration of the archaic clan system. Instead of restoring the classless democracy of the past, it moved in precisely the opposite direction. The development of commerce and industry dissolved away the residues of the old kinship bonds, introducing a democracy of slaves and slave-owners, a democracy in which the 'people' themselves were a ruling class.

Even Lewis Morgan, who was fascinated by the 'liberty, equality and fraternity' of the ancient clans, was confused. He describes the new political system founded by Kleisthenes as a 'pure democracy' with an antiquity as great 'as the gentes themselves': an improved version of the democratic ideas which had existed from time immemorial. But the new system was founded, of course, not simply as Morgan says, on territory and property but upon slavery too. The 'atrocious slavery', which marred Roman attempts to 'recover the ancient principles of democracy', marred Greek efforts as well (1964, p. 219; p. 268). The new democracy was a form of the state. It was structured around an institution monopolising legitimate coercion. It was rooted in slavery and (as we have seen) imperialism. If there was an element of continuity with the past, there was also a profound and radical rupture.

We have already argued that the rise of liberalism exacerbates the problem of getting to grips with democracy. It is now possible to see why. If liberalism mystifies the concept of democracy, it is because, as we shall see, it mystifies the question of the state. The ambiguity of democracy is ultimately the ambiguity of politics and power, for how can it be said that the 'people' rule when government expresses itself through the legitimate force of political hierarchy?

Both conservatives and democrats in Greece were bemused by this problem. Democrats mistook the new statist democracy for the old communal democracy of tribal times, while conservatives feared that there was nothing (in theory at any rate) to stop the principle of liberty and equality from going to extremes. Morgan exclaimed enthusiastically that 'the Athenians were able to carry forward their ideas of government to their logical results' (1964, p. 219)—but this is precisely what did *not* happen. Democracy became a form of the state based upon repressive hierarchy and class exploitation. Its theoretical form concealed its practical content—hence its chronic liability to confuse.

John Cotton, a New England divine of the seventeenth century, once declared democracy to be the meanest and worst of all forms of government. If the people governed, he protested, over *whom* were they to rule? It is said (by H.G. Wells) that when the supreme ruler of the moon was told that governments exist on earth in which everybody rules, he immediately ordered the application of cooling sprays to his brow! Democracy begins its long history of generating Gladstone bags and proliferating confusions and clouds of humbug when it embraces the state.

It is here that the roots of our problems lie.

8 The Subversive Abstractions of the Liberal Tradition

THE POLITICAL ARTEFACT AND THE ABSTRACT INDIVIDUAL

We have argued so far that once the concept of democracy is conceived as a form of the state—as an expression of hierarchical power—then an element of ambiguity inevitably creeps in. At the same time it needs to be emphasised that in the ancient (as in the medieval) world, this ambiguity is only latent and embryonic. It is true that conservatives can claim that democracy threatens to obliterate all social divisions while democrats confuse a statist system with the clan structures of ancestral times, but on the whole Greek writers make it clear that democracy is an egalitarian and participatory government for free male citizens. It is a form of the state which explicitly excludes women, slaves and resident aliens.

The point about slavery and the other social hierarchies is that they are deemed *natural* in character. This is the real significance of Aristotle's famous dictum about 'men' as 'political animals'. It is not simply that humans are social by nature: it is that the *state* itself 'belongs to a class of objects which exist in nature' (1962, p. 28). It is impossible, in other words, to conceive of people living outside social and political relationships. Hence the conservative argument that democracy dissolves away the hierarchies of 'nature' cannot be taken too seriously, for if (as even the Greek democrats acknowledge) people are naturally divided into rulers and ruled, then a world in which *all* govern becomes a conceptual impossibility.

The ancient Greeks are famous for thinking in concrete terms. People play specific social and political roles: they do not exist simply as 'individuals'. The concept of the individual (it has been said with some chagrin) is 'a tiresome modern abstraction which might almost be designed to mislead'. Students of Greek thought are fortunate in the fact that this 'obfuscating' notion rarely appears in antiquity, and indeed can hardly be expressed in Greek, or for that matter in Latin (De Ste Croix, 1981, p. 439). As Hegel was fond of saying, the Greeks did not really know 'man as such' (1956, p. 18; p. 254).

Broadly speaking, the same can also be said of the medieval world. It is true that writers like Aquinas are committed as Christians to a belief in equality since every human being is created by a common divinity. Yet this egalitarianism is confined to our existence before the Fall. Once the Fall occurs, humans are corrupted by nature and sin ('the mother of servitude'), and thus, with medieval Christians as with the Greeks, people divide into citizens and slaves, men and women, etc. in the time-honoured 'natural' way. A world in which people govern themselves without a state is unthinkable, and Aquinas follows Aristotle's view of democracy as a regime of liberty 'dominated' by the populace (Bigongiari, 1953, p. xxv). As long as the state and hierarchical social power appears to be natural, definitions of democracy remain relatively concrete.

What exacerbates the kind of embyronic ambiguities noted in the concluding section of the last chapter is the rise of liberalism. It is this development above all which now makes it possible for democracy to begin its long conceptual career as the purveyor of mystification and humbug. But why should this be? The classical liberals were not democrats, and we have already noted for example the grave reservations which the American Founding Fathers expressed on the subject. Indeed virtually two millennia have to pass before democracy as a positive (and not a pejorative) political term reappears in any Western European language (Dunn, 1979, p. 6). Yet this is our point. If liberals before, say, 1780 did not consider themselves democrats, the creed they *did* espouse has subversive implications which appear far more dramatic than anything which has come down to us from the democratic ideologies of the ancient world.

It has been estimated that when the US Declaration of Independence was proclaimed in 1776, there were living in the rebellious colonies some 650,000 slaves, 250,000 indentured servants and 300,000 Indians—roughly forty per cent of the total population. In addition, of course, women in general were excluded from participating in government (Hoffman, 1983, p. 62). The hand which wrote the historic Declaration also wrote advertisements for fugitives, and in South Carolina human chattels were actually given as bounty to soldiers volunteering for the revolutionary cause. Unsurprisingly, thousands of slaves fought on the side of the British.

But why should these exclusions seem problematic? The Declaration, it could be argued, made the case for popular sovereignty as a form of the state, and the state by definition implies a division between rulers and ruled. In 1776 women, slaves, Indians and indentured servants were part of the 'ruled'. They were 'subjects' rather than citizens, and, as Rousseau insisted, only those who use the word 'citizen' exclusively understand the real meaning of the term (1968, p. 61). Indeed, the Declarations of Rights proclaimed in Mississippi and Alabama (in 1817 and 1819) refer quite explicitly to 'freemen' as the recipients of equal rights.

Yet the remarkable feature of the Declaration of Independence is of course that it says that 'all men' have rights which are 'unalienable'. These rights derive from the 'Laws of Nature and Nature's God', and they depend neither on society nor the state for their recognition. They are the independent property of individuals themselves, individuals as such, individuals in the abstract. This is why the 'rights of man' doctrine not only alarmed royalists and reactionaries: it also unnerved some of the liberals as well. The eleven years which intervened between the Declaration and the Constitution were turbulent ones, punctuated by protest and rebellion by debtors and small farmers, mechanics and artisans agitating for greater equality. Charles Beard in a famous tract in 1913 branded the Constitution a 'counter-revolutionary' document on the grounds that, as the work of a monied and slave-owning elite, it had betrayed the radical promise of the Declaration of Independence by placing property above rights.

It is certainly a striking feature of the Constitution that it makes no reference to the natural rights doctrine. Hamilton who had once spoken lyrically of rights 'written as with a sunbeam in the whole volume of human nature' now spoke darkly of insurrections, seditions and doctrinaire metaphysics—'the reveries of those political doctors whose sagacity disdains the admonitions of experimental instruction' (1961, p. 178). Asserting rights in nature can be a dangerous business. It might push people to 'extremes', and although none of the rebellious debtors, dirt farmers or ship calkers had, during those turbulent eleven years, raised either the question of slavery, women's rights or justice for the indigenous Indians, they were still denounced in lurid terms. In the memorable words of one conservative attack at the time, they stood exposed as 'Democrats Unveiled or Tyrants Stripped of the Garb of Patriotism' (Gettell, 1928, p. 121).

The rebels of the 1780s may not have been democrats but they *were* radicals, and, like all radicals in the late eighteenth century, they took the natural rights doctrine as their starting point. As late as 1895, D.G. Ritchie could still complain that the theory was capable of mischief (he particularly had the anarchists in mind). It appealed from 'institution to individual judgment'. Its individualism had a marked 'negativity' to it, a critical 'abstractedness' able to push to one side the 'concrete facts of social life and history' (1895, p. 14). After all, if nature itself had declared humans equal, then repressive governments and social hierarchies the world over were vulnerable to conceptual attack. The Fall, which had enabled medieval theorists to reconcile Christianity with ancient Greek thought, lost its theoretical significance as freedom and happiness were substituted for the vale of tears.

This is why the liberals made their opponents (and sometimes even themselves) so nervous. Hobbes's *Leviathan* is a case in point. One might have thought that Hobbes's arguments for an absolutist state would have been popular among the royalists during the civil war. After all, he had supported them politically. Yet if Hobbes was a conservative, he was no Aristotelian, Bees, he tells us, may be 'numbered' amongst the 'Political creatures' but people are not. Distinctions between master and servant are purely conventional in character, for there are few so foolish that would not rather govern themselves than be governed by others (1968, p. 225; p. 211). Nature hath made 'men' equal. The state is an artefact which rests upon consent. It is true that Hobbes constructed a theory that was far more authoritarian than anything subsequent liberals could accept. But the postulates of this theory were still egalitarian in their abstract logic, and hence his arguments were never really acceptable in royalist circles.

Locke was even less inclined than Hobbes to call himself a democrat. He took it for granted that voters were men, merchants and landowners—property owners of patriarchal 'substance'. The question of universal suffrage, even of male universal suffrage, is not even raised in his *Two Treatises of Government*. Yet the theory rests upon an abstract egalitarianism. Locke *does* say that all are born to the same advantage; all are equal without subordination and subjection, and all remain in this state of natural equality for as long as they wish (1924, p. 118; p. 124).

Like his fellow liberals, he attacked the argument that the state resembles a family with a paternal king ruling over juvenile subjects. There is nothing natural, Locke insists, about hierarchy and the state. It is only the subordination of humans to their 'omnipotent and infinitely wise Maker' which cannot change. In the light of assumptions like these, it is not difficult to understand why Locke's conservative critics should sneer, in the words of one John Leslie, 'Would they send men about to poll the whole nation?' (Dunn, 1979, p. 4). They might have missed the finer points of Locke's (distinctly hierarchical) doctrine of consent, but about one thing conservatives were clear. Natural equality; the state as an artefact; an inalienable right to rebel; all this sounded suspiciously like a demand for democracy!

A hapless King Charles was to reproach the English parliamentarians (who had taken him prisoner) for 'the illegal proceedings of them that presume from servants to become masters and labour to bring in democracy' (Dunn, 1979, p. 3). Yet it is abundantly clear that 'bringing in democracy' was not their intention. If a commonwealth must needs suffer, Cromwell had declared, it should rather suffer from rich men rather than poor men. His puritan gentry attacked the left wing of the movement—the Levellers—in precisely the same terms in which Charles had attacked the parliamentarians: for seeking to turn servants against masters and the poor against the rich. Moreover it should be noted that even the radical Levellers were not really democrats, although historians disagree as to the precise categories of 'servants' and 'paupers' they wished to exclude from the franchise.

Once again it was the abstract logic of liberal theory which had raised the spectre of democracy. Cromwell's son-in-law Ireton could object that if the law of nature is held to be supreme over all constitutions, he 'would fain have any man shew me where you will end'. Liberty cannot be provided for 'in a general sense' if property is to be preserved (Ritchie, 1895, p. 10; Hill, 1969, p. 120). Charles himself made the point which worried the more conservative puritans. He desired the people's liberty and freedom as much as anyone, he insisted, but 'I must tell you that their liberty and freedom consists in having of government'. A subject and a sovereign are 'clear different things' (Dunn, 1979, p. 3).

Take away the 'naturalness' of government; postulate people as equals; demand rule by consent—and you undermine the basis of all political order. Democracy appears as the impossible result. It is during the historic upheavals that gave birth to the modern world that we encounter liberal abstractions in their most startlingly subversive form.

THE THEOLOGICAL NICETIES OF CLASSICAL LIBERALISM

We have noted that before the 1780s the term democracy was generally used as a word of abuse. It was a concept hurled at liberals (and radicals in particular) by conservatives who feared the subversive implications of the natural rights doctrine. After all, if hierarchies and the state were not 'natural', then what established order was safe from attack? Natural rights implied anarchy, and the concept of democracy seemed an appropriate word to encapsulate conservative anxieties and fears.

But it does not follow of course that because conservatives denounced liberal abstractions as democratic, this is an accurate characterisation of their social and political content. On the contrary, the more closely we examine these abstractions, the more curious they become. In particular, we cannot help noting that these abstractions appear to embody a schizophrenic conflict between what they appear to promise in theory, and what they lead to in practice. Ireton, for example, saw in liberal abstractions not merely the danger of democracy but even the spectre of communism. But if natural rights doctrine *was* as subversive as conservatives imagined, then why do we find classical liberals invariably supporting a property-owning society of a more or less elitist kind?

This point is raised sharply to Tocqueville, who is fascinated by (what he calls) the Americans' 'aptitude and taste for general ideas'. Unlike the Greeks and Romans (or more aristocratic peoples like the English), the Americans, Tocqueville argues, display an 'injudicious warmth' for making generalisations (1966, p. 564), and he ascribes this craving for abstraction to a belief in equality. The movement towards equality appears to be universal and permanent, a force daily passing beyond human control—a blind instrument 'in the hands of God'. Where, he asks, will it end? Does anyone imagine that democracy, which has destroyed the feudal system and vanquished kings, will fall back before the middle class and the rich (1966, p. 8)?

An intriguing comment which raises a number of testing questions. If democracy is a radical and unstoppable movement towards ever greater equality, why is it that in America (the land of democracy *par excellence*) property rights are so keenly defended. Tocqueville, as we noted earlier, is emphatic on this point. If maxims called democratic in France cause outrage in the United States, then this suggests that the Americans *do* imagine (in fact they insist) that democracy *does* fall short of an attack on the middle class and the rich.

A second problem arises. It is true that property ownership in Tocqueville's America was uniquely widespread, but was this enough to make America democratic? What in particular had happened to that forty per cent of the population—the slaves, Indians and indentured servants (not to mention the disenfranchised women) who were around when the Declaration of Independence itself was signed?

Tocqueville says nothing about indentured servants or votes for women. He does, however, devote a whole chapter to the problems facing the Indians and the blacks, and his analysis is scathing. 'In one blow', he writes, 'oppression has deprived the descendants of the Africans of almost all the privileges of humanity'. As for the indigenous Indians, they have been subject to the tyranny of government and the 'greed of the colonists'. In a particularly poignant sentence, he comments: 'Seeing what happens in the world, might not one say that the European is to men of other races what man is to the animals? He makes them serve his convenience, and when he cannot bend them to his will he destroys them' (1966, p. 392).

Now the implications of all this are hardly less than startling for an analysis of democracy in America. Tocqueville quotes a Cherokee petition to the Congress: 'our fathers never consented to a treaty whose result was to deprive them of their most sacred rights and to rob them of their country' (1966, p. 420)—and he notes the truth of this contention. How does this square then with the American love of generalisations about equality and human rights? How is tyranny, oppression and even a kind of 'liberal' genocide—'it is impossible to destroy men with more respect to the laws of humanity' (1966, p. 421)—compatible with democracy and egalitarian beliefs? In what sense is democracy in America democracy at all?

Tocqueville not only emphasises the abstract character of American ideas, but also falls victim unfortunately to the very abstractions he seeks to criticise. For although he does provide a scathing critique of the racial policy of his day, he speaks of the position of blacks and Indians as 'tangents to my subject'. Strictly speaking, these people stand *outside* the analysis of America as 'an immense and complete democracy' (1966, p. 390). But how can this be? Slavery was integral to the political mores of the South and to the US economy as a whole. Racism was a central component of the Jacksonian 'democracy'. Without the enslavement of the blacks and the expropriation of Indian lands, how is one to explain America's celebrated 'restlessness amid prosperity'—the 'egalitarian' psychology and institutions of the country itself?

In short, liberal abstractions may strike conservatives as subversive, but, as we can see from Tocqueville's own analysis, they are not to be taken on trust. A humanity united in theory is divided in practice. Conquest, robbery, exploitation and expropriation: all occur in the name of natural rights and the equality of 'man'. To say simply that liberals do not practice what they preach is not enough. We need to go further and ask whether there is not something inherently mystifying about liberal abstractions themselves, so that their egalitarian promise necessarily turns into its hierarchical opposite?

To answer this question, we must pose another. How is it possible for liberal abstractions to arise in the first place? What made it possible for liberal thinkers to imagine that individuals *can* actually exist in a state of nature—in a state of wholesale abstraction from society itself? The abstract individuals of classical liberal theory certainly have readily identifiable human traits. They are portrayed as acting rationally with a well-developed sense of their own self-interest. Yet, to make the most obvious of objections, how can individuals do anything at all, rational or otherwise, if they are apparently suspended in a social vacuum?

It is the character of this 'rational activity' which gives us a clue. Locke, for example, has his abstract individuals *exchanging* goods and services in the state of nature, and these acts of exchange furnish the key to our riddle. For what is it about the exchange process which makes it appear that individuals can act together while still remaining completely apart? What kind of activity is it that mystifies its own relational character, its very existence as a social relationship? The exchange process which appears straightforward enough on the surface, bristles, as we shall now see, with 'metaphysical subtleties and theological niceties'—with problems of a thoroughly mystifying kind (Marx, 1970, p. 73). It is only by getting to grips with (at least some of) these subtleties and niceties that we can begin to explain the subversive abstractions of the liberal tradition.

Our abstract individuals exchange objects which they have independently appropriated or produced. But for objects to exchange (i.e. to exist as commodities), each must have a value equal to the other, and here right away we encounter a problem which had defeated the best minds of Greek antiquity. How can objects be equated (made the same) when they are different—when they may resemble each other as little (to take one of Marx's examples) as boot boxes and palaces?

To exchange, commodities must have something in common. What they have in common is the labour which, as Locke says, individuals mix in with the objects they appropriate. But products all differ because the labour of their producers is different. Some plough; some cut; others sew. It follows therefore that different commodities can exchange only if the different kinds of labour which produce them can be equated. Here we come to our crunch point. Goods can only exchange as commodities if the labour embodied in them is, as Marx stresses, abstract and homogeneous in character. Those who exchange commodities have to calculate the value of the objects they exchange in terms of a 'socially necessary labour time' which puts out of sight the particular qualities of this or that form of labour involved. Productive energies are of necessity reduced to 'human labour in the abstract' (1970, p. 38).

This is what makes the commodity as a good produced for exchange such a bizarre phenomenon. The value which it embodies is abstract. Not 'an atom of matter', as Marx puts it, 'enters into its composition' (1970, p. 47). This value converts every product into a 'social hieroglyphic' because it conceals the particular kind of human labour needed to produce it. It conceals, in other words, the social character of the productive process. A definite social relationship between people appears in the fantastic form of a relation between things (Marx, 1970, p. 72).

Not only are commodities 'abstract': so too are the individuals who exchange them. As Jordan comments (1985, p. 167), the price mechanism acts as a 'polite cloak' for all 'the tragedies and triumphs, unlucky losses or dishonest gains' which lead the participants into the market place, willingly or unwillingly, to exchange their goods. When buyers and sellers meet, their activity is regulated by the accidental and ever-fluctuating relations of exchange between products. The social activity of individuals appears to them as 'the action of objects', since individuals make contact only when they exchange 'things'. Products dominate the producers. Individuals confront one another as persons whose will resides in the objects they exchange (Marx, 1970, p. 84).

The key to this analysis is to be found in the concept of abstraction, a concept which usefully complements the concepts of concentration and coercion employed in earlier sections of this book. For abstraction is not merely an activity of the mind: it is also a practical process of equation which makes commodity exchanges both possible, and yet, at the same time, highly mystifying. The concept of abstraction enables us to explain why Locke and the classical liberals of the seventeenth and eighteenth century could imagine that individuals can exist in splendid isolation from one another in a state of nature while continuing to trade as market partners.

This mystification enters into the very institution of contract as a relationship between two independent agents, each autonomous of the other. Hence even the formation of society and the state appears as a 'social contract', as a product of exchange—an act of prior consent. The only force which stands above these abstract individuals is the impersonal workings of the market—the theological laws of a supreme nature—so that, as both Marx and Tocqueville stress in their different ways, the classical liberal view of the individual translates very easily into religious terms.

We are now in a position to decode more comprehensively the hieroglyphic abstractions of the liberal tradition. The abstract individual is conceivable only if we picture individuals as owners of commodities confronting one another in the market place. But these sales and purchases involve more than may appear at first sight. For the accumulation of commodities cannot get off the ground as an expanding and dynamic process if people are simply selling in order to buy. Merchants and traders are needed who will buy in order to sell. But how are they to make a profit?

Cheating, windfalls and 'cornering the market' cannot in themselves explain what Marx calls 'the never-ending augmentation of exchange-value' (1970, p. 153). Money bags, as Marx puts it, must find a commodity able to generate more value than it itself possesses. This of course is the commodity of labour power, the productive capacity of 'free' labourers who are doubly 'independent' and 'abstract' as individuals. Independent of others, they can freely sign contracts on their own behalf, and, independent of any private means, they must sell their labour power in order to survive. Hence in both Locke and Hobbes (as Macpherson, 1962, has rightly argued) the abstraction of the individual implies not merely market exchanges between inanimate commodities but the exploitation of wage labour. Thus, as we have seen, the very postulate of the abstract individual points to radical inequalities in the real world.

But these radical inequalities do not stop here. Capitalist accumulation presupposes that massive quantities of 'mercantile capital' have been acquired through colonial conquest; peasants are driven from the land through enclosures; aboriginal populations are uprooted; and, in Marx's memorable phrase, the African continent is turned into a 'warren for commercial hunting of black skins'. The 'veiled slavery of the wage-workers in Europe' requires for its pedestal 'slavery pure and simple in the New World (1970, p. 751; pp. 759–60). Without conquest, enslavement, robbery and the most direct use of force, there can be no capitalists and labourers. The presence of both as 'abstract individuals' necessarily implies a history of expropriation written in letters of fire and blood (1970, p. 715).

Nor can we forget the hierarchical family in which, as Locke comments (1924, p. 157), the man 'naturally' emerges as the 'stronger and abler'. Just as the worker freely consents to the sale of labour power, so a woman freely consents to marry a man with economic supremacy. Within the family of liberal patriarchy the husband is the bourgeois and the wife 'represents the proletariat' (Engels, 1972, p. 137). Since property considerations prevail over personal qualities, the monogamous family has prostitution and adultery as its necessary concomitants.

In other words, the more closely we examine classical liberal abstractions, the less benevolent they become. They appear subversive to conservatives, but when analysed carefully, they imply, as we have argued above, a whole spectrum of social and statist hierarchies ranging from patriarchy to outright slavery. This is why Locke, the most 'classic' of all the liberals, finds it necessary to stress that the power of a magistrate over a subject must be distinguished from 'that of a father over his children, a master over his servant, a husband over his wife and a lord over his slave' (1924, p. 118). Conservatives need have no fear that this is a theory prone to anarchist extremes. The exercise of natural rights brings into play (as Locke's own theory shows) the use of money, the accumulation of capital and the existence of a propertyless proletariat. It justifies the 'natural' subordination of women to men and the ownership of slaves.

This point cannot but compel us to reconsider the whole relationship between liberalism and democracy. For in what sense can it be said that the natural rights tradition is democratic when it necessarily presupposes rule by a patriarchal and propertied elite? Only those who fall victim to the metaphysical subtleties and theological niceties of the liberal tradition can really imagine that its abstractions are democratic at all.

CAN LIBERALS BECOME DEMOCRATS? ENGAGING MACPHERSON

We have argued so far what makes liberalism so mystifying is that its subversive premises are abstract. They appear to imply democracy (indeed even communism), thus moving conservatives to indignation and horror. But because these subversive premises are *abstractions* rooted in the metaphysical subtleties and theological niceties of commodity production, they are organically tied to the rise of capitalism and to all the radical inequalities of power which this system presupposes. Hence when the classical liberals insisted that they were not democrats, they should be taken at their word.

By the nineteenth century, however, liberals begin to seek some kind of *rapprochement* with democracy, indeed so much so that by the twentieth century, they are noisily proclaiming (in the words of the notorious T.D. Weldon) that 'democracy', 'capitalism' and 'liberalism' are all alternative names for the same thing (1953, p. 86). Where there had once been fierce opposition, now a blissful harmony reigns. But how is it possible for so dramatic a transformation to take place?

To explore this problem further, it is profitable at this point to engage the arguments of C.B. Macpherson, for Macpherson has applied himself with great industry and scholarship to the task of effecting a synthesis between liberalism and democracy: a synthesis which acknowledges the tension between our two concepts while laying the basis for harmony. Our differences with Macpherson will shortly emerge, but there is no doubt that his argument provides critical insights into the ambiguities and complexities of this troubled conceptual relationship.

As we have seen, liberals right up until the last two decades of the eighteenth century were clearly not democrats, and they declined to present themselves as though they were. How then did the transition from liberalism to democracy take place? If Macpherson is to succeed in constructing a viable synthesis between our two concepts, it is with this 'transformation' problem that our analysis must begin.

Democratic visions have continually recurred for over 2,000 years, and Macpherson contrasts what he calls the 'one class model' of the ancient world (a model which was also endorsed by Rousseau and Jefferson) with the 'class-divided' models of liberal democracy. But this characterisation is confusing for two reasons. The first is that class itself is a category of *division*, and if the poor ruled in say ancient Athens, this was because there were women, aliens and slaves whom they ruled *over*. A 'one class model' implies a division between classes. It is true that in the case of Rousseau and Jefferson (Macpherson also gives the example of the Levellers), concrete social analysis had given way to the abstract visions of the natural rights tradition. But the fact remains that none of these 'one-class' democrats supported the case for universal suffrage. All excluded women. All excluded 'dependents', however these were defined. As radicals, Rousseau, Jefferson and the Levellers may have looked towards a society in which citizens were independent proprietors, but this 'ideal' itself pre-supposed (as we have seen) slavery, colonial expropriation, patriarchy and wage labour.

This brings me to my second point. If 'one class democrats' subscribed, as Macpherson points out, to a 'vision' of democracy which did not embrace the political community as a whole (1977, p. 10), is it correct to describe this vision as 'democratic' at all? Rousseau might condemn slavery as contrary to nature—yet he could still wonder whether there are not some situations in which 'the citizen can be perfectly free only if the slave is absolutely a slave' (1968, p. 143). Jefferson was also compromised by slavery, and the Declaration of Independence (which he drafted) has little sympathy for the 'merciless Indian savages' whom the colonists have robbed of their land. Even the Levellers were tempted by Cromwell's plantations across the sea in Ireland. The point is that the 'property-owning' ideal implies an historic process of expropriation, and however much 'one class democrats' may have regretted, for example, the development of wage labour, all these exclusions flow logically from the abstract premises of the model. To characterise this model simply as 'democratic' must therefore be open to some question.

This point can be strengthened only by the fact that until the late eighteenth century, the question of democracy (as we have seen) is not an issue for liberals anyway. It becomes an issue only when those who are excluded from political power as the victims of liberal abstractions begin to demand their rights. The putative conversion of liberals to democrats starts with James Mill and Jeremy Bentham, and hence it seems odd to refer to previous thinkers as 'one class democrats' when in fact they were liberals (or ancients) who took class divisions for granted.

In the case of Bentham and the elder Mill, support for universal male suffrage was, as Macpherson points out, grudging and cautious. Bentham had initially favoured a limited franchise which would have excluded the poor and the uneducated (in addition to women). But in a Europe radicalised by the French Revolution, some British liberals at least had become conscious of the need to cultivate popular support if the old Whig oligarchy of landed and financial interests was to be displaced. Hence Bentham concludes by 1820 that while he would happily settle for a limited householder franchise, this would not really satisfy those excluded—who perhaps constitute 'a majority of male adults' (Macpherson, 1977, p. 35).

Mill's 'conversion' to democracy is similarly cautious. Indeed what is remarkable about Mill's *Essay on Government* (1828) is that he asserts that all need to have the vote in order to protect properly their interests, and yet then proceeds to argue that these interests could be adequately secured even if all women, all men under forty, and the poorest third of the male population over forty were excluded from the vote. Unsurprisingly, Macpherson describes Mill (like Bentham) as 'less than a whole-hearted democrat' (1977, p. 39). But in what sense can it be said that he and Bentham were democrats at all?

To answer this question, we must explore the impact which an explicit recognition of class divisions makes upon the subversive abstractions of the liberal tradition. For what is striking about the utilitarian argument for democracy is that the belief in natural rights has now been abandoned. This has a two-fold significance.

It indicates firstly that by the nineteenth century, liberals have become more conservative than their classical forebears. They reject the revolutionary notion that the 'people' have inalienable rights which no oppressor can remove. We have already noted a similar kind of nervousness during the English Civil War and in the period following the American Declaration of Independence. Jacobin radicalism during the French Revolution once again underlined the subversive nature of the natural rights tradition. On the basis of the natural rights argument Paine and Godwin had begun to push liberalism in the direction of social democracy and anarchism, so that by appealing to 'utility' rather than 'rights'—to 'experience' rather than 'nature'—the utilitarians believed that they were presenting a 'respectable' rather than a revolutionary case for political change.

But what is also revealing about the movement away from natural rights is that it suggests that the abstraction of the individual—central to the classical liberal tradition—has become increasingly difficult to sustain. All the evidence now points to the fact that class divisions are not a pathology to be avoided but a social reality which is here to stay. Bentham himself notes that the great mass of citizens are condemned to live at a basic subsistence level, having no other resource except their daily industry (Macpherson, 1977, p. 28; Jordan, 1985, p. 66). Given deprivations such as these, in what sense can it be said that the ranks of the propertied and the propertyless are both composed of 'abstract individuals' all pursuing pleasure and avoiding pain in the same old time-honoured way?

It is true that utilitarianism remains militantly abstract, and James Mill can still find in Hobbes a writer whose reasonings are difficult to 'controvert'. But the move away from the postulate of inalienable rights signals an acceptance of the fact that what divides individuals is becoming as important as that which unites them. After all, the utilitarian pursuit of the greatest happiness of the greatest number may well imply (as critics have been quick to point out) a radically divided community whose conflicts of interest require positive intervention from the state to sort out. The truth is that in accepting the division of society into classes as natural and inevitable, the utilitarians had begun to subvert the abstract universality of their own premises.

Injected into the context of capitalist hierarchies, the famous felicity principle runs into trouble. Consider the following problem. According to Bentham, the incentive to produce arises from the desire to avoid the pain of starvation, and to enjoy the pleasure of abundance. In a mythical world of abstract individuals all naturally equal in their endowments, this principle holds for 'all'. However, in what Bentham himself accepts is a class-divided society, capitalists are cushioned against the fear of starvation, and workers, no matter how hard they work, have virtually no chance of acquiring abundance. They, as Bentham says, will always be near 'indigence'. In other words, there are now two orders of individuals who have little in common. One enjoys the pleasure while the other suffers the pain.

What then of the 'equality' which the utilitarian legislator supposedly favours? If all have the same capacity for pleasure, and 'each portion of wealth has a corresponding portion of happiness', then maximising happiness should logically require that all have equal wealth. The division of individuals into classes, however, makes this problematic. Hence we find Bentham arguing that the 'quantum of sensibility' (i.e. the capacity for pleasure) appears geater in the 'higher ranks of men' than in the lower. The implication is clear: the poor need far less wealth to make them happy than the rich. While Bentham postulates that the end of the law is to 'provide subsistence; to produce abundance; to favour equality; to maintain security', he also insists that when security of property comes into conflict with equality, it is equality which 'yields' (Macpherson, 1977, p. 30; Jordan, 1985, p. 66).

All this is most revealing. It suggests that once liberal abstractions are concretely analysed, they simply disintegrate. The doctrine of the greatest happiness of the greatest number, which appears egalitarian and individualistic, collapses into a doctrine in which abundance for the few means bare subsistence for the many. Equality yields to property. It is not utility or happiness which is to be maximised: it is wealth. This explicit recognition of class divisions has the effect, that is to say, of bringing liberal abstractions down to earth. Conflicts of class interest can no longer be buried in a world of metaphysical abstractions. After all, the dispossessed are beginning to organise themselves and demand some of their rights, thus confronting the utilitarian liberals with a serious dilemma.

On the one hand, it can no longer be assumed that all individuals are (in some abstract sense) the 'same'. Natural rights theory has become both dangerous, and, in its classical liberal form, highly implausible. On the other hand, if society is deeply divided along class lines, will not conceding the vote simply enable the rich to be expropriated by the poor? Will it not bring about the kind of 'tyranny of the majority' against which the more conservative American republicans had already warned?

Mill and Bentham's response to this problem is an interesting one. Bentham moves to the principle of one male one vote (as Macpherson himself points out) only when he has become convinced that the poor will not use their votes to level or destroy property. Mill is even more forthright. On acquiring the vote, the vast majority of the working class will, he says, merely follow the advice and example of 'the middle rank'—that class in society which gives to science, art and legislation itself 'their most distinguished ornaments', and which is the chief source of all that is 'refined and exalted in human nature' (Lively and Rees, 1978, p. 94). The business of government is properly the business of the rich, and the only 'good means' of obtaining this government is through 'the free suffrage of the people' (Macpherson 1977, p. 42).

We are now in a position to assess Macpherson's contention that the utilitarians provided the first historical model of a 'liberal democracy'—for his difficulty is this. If Mill and Bentham were democrats, we would expect them to support the extension of power to the people. Yet not only do they both exclude women from the suffrage, but they make it clear that votes are to be handed to male workers in the expectation that political rights will not be used to alter the existing distribution of property. This expectation must surely throw some light upon Mill and Bentham's democratic credentials.

The classical liberals were fully conscious of the fact that property brings with it not only social power but political power as well. Indeed, as Macpherson has argued elsewhere, the liberal tradition from Hobbes to Mill understood power in extractive terms: as the capacity, in James Mill's words, to render the persons and properties of human beings subservient to our pleasures (1973, p. 42). But this must imply that extractive power is basically rooted in property, for what 'extractive power' can be enjoyed in a market society by those who have no capital or land? Thus on the basis of James Mill's own argument, if all the capital in a society is owned by ten per cent of the population, then each of the owners has on average an extractive power equivalent to virtually all the powers of nine other people (1973, p. 44). Macpherson unfavourably contrasts this analysis with that of later theorists who drive a wedge between property and political power, and thus move away from the classical liberal contention that owning property as capital gives you political as well as social clout.

There can be little doubt (as Macpherson himself emphasises) that both Mill and Bentham supported the franchise as a way of 'protecting' the rights of property. It is true that the 'model' alarmed more conservative liberals like Macaulay, who declared rather extravagantly that in a democracy of the kind 'Mr Mill' proposes, the rich would be pillaged as unmercifully as under a Turkish Lord (Lively and Rees, 1978, p. 120). Yet nothing could have been further from Mill's thoughts. Like Bentham, he advocated adult male suffrage in the belief that government would remain the 'business of the rich', and that under the circumstances, a 'protective democracy' was actually the *best* way of defending the interests of capital.

Mill was not of course unaware of the problems which might arise with 'the occasional turbulence of a manufacturing district' where the population consisted almost entirely of rich manufacturers and impoverished workers. But he remained confident that most people would be guided by the virtuous middle rank, and one reason for this optimism was his assumption that the middle rank in Britain constituted a large portion of the population as a whole (Lively and Rees, 1978, p. 94). In this it might well be argued that he had under-estimated the depth to which the industrial revolution was polarising society in Britain. There was, however, another reason why he and Bentham might have thought that workers would naturally accept middle class hegemony.

Bentham had pointed to the USA as a country in which the poor did not use their political rights to undermine property, even though this capacity was 'within the compass of their legal power' (Mapherson, 1977, p. 37). On the face of it, this example seems less than helpful to Bentham's argument for a 'protective democracy' since, as Macaulay was quick to point out, conditions in the USA were exceptional and could soon change (Lively and Rees, 1978, p. 121). Yet the implications of Bentham's remark are profound.

They suggest a fertile linkage between the 'egalitarianism' of the labour contract and the 'egalitarianism' of a 'protective democracy'. In the contract between capitalist and worker, each exchanges equivalent for equivalent—wages for labour power. The *law*, in enforcing this contract, thereby upholds the formal equality which necessarily exists between the two parties. Of course in reality, as Marx argued, the capitalist has a social power which effecively compels the worker to enter the market but the law knows nothing of these underlying inequalities. A legal right, in other words, might provide an unreliable guide to a person's real power but it creates nevertheless a powerful 'juridical illusion' that people enter into contracts freely and as equals.

Why should the democratic franchise not operate in precisely the same way? Adult workers are given the vote, but guided by the 'advice and example' of the virtuous middle rank they use this vote to confirm rather than challenge an established order in which, as Mill says, 'government' is properly the business of the rich'. They have the 'legal power' to run their own lives—just as in the capital-labour contract they have 'legal equality' with their employers. But in both cases there is no little hypocrisy and deception involved. In the macrocosm of politics as in the microcosom of the capital-labour relationship, power remains firmly in the hands of those who own property.

In what sense can it be said then that Bentham and Mill had constructed a protective model of a liberal *democracy*? If, as Macpherson himself concedes, power equates broadly with property, then the 'protective democracy' of Mill and Bentham is a partial democracy indeed. It gives *rights* to the poor but does it give them power?

What Easton calls the 'schizoid malady' of abstract liberalism (1949, p. 18) takes on a new and more comprehensive form: it concedes democracy in theory only to deny it in practice. It concedes majority rights (at least to all males) on the understanding that these rights will not be used to challenge minority *power*. The conversion of liberals to democracy is therefore much more problematic than Macpherson seems to think. True, the abstract equalities of the legal world have now been extended to the political realm as part of that subversive logic conservatives had always feared. But, as we have already seen, liberalism's subversive abstractions are subversive *abstractions*. If they terrify conservatives, they also conceal quite dramatic inequalities of power beneath their benevolent protestations of rights.

Hence when legal rights are projected into the political realm, and the 'social contract' now embraces those without property as well, it is surely naive to assume that this signals the simple transformation of liberalism into democracy. Much has to be done, as we shall see, before the democracy of abstract forms can become a democracy of social reality.

J.S. MILL AND THE OLD LIBERALISM

The utilitarians had begun to recognise (if only implicitly) that a liberal capitalist society is composed of two radically different orders of 'abstract individuals'. Yet these individuals, though divided, still had enough in common to make a 'protective democracy' a practical proposition. Those without property would not use their vote to challenge the prerogatives of government as the business of the rich. It was of course this sanguine assumption which Macaulay attacked, and it was an attack which gave a youthful John Stuart Mill 'much to think about' (J.S. Mill, 1964, p. 121).

It was clear to most British liberals by about the middle of the nineteenth century that class divisions were continuing to deepen. As he read the Mill-Macaulay debate, the younger Mill had already begun to wonder whether his father was correct in asserting that 'an identity of interest' between the governing body and the community at large could be secured 'by the mere conditions of election' (1964, p. 122). After all (as J.S. Mill comments in 1848) the working classes themselves are showing, through their support for trade unions and for Chartism, that they see the interests of their employers as 'not identical with their own, but opposite to them' (Macpherson, 1977, p. 45). What divides 'individuals' has become more important than what unites them, and the real problem with Benthamite utilitarianism—as Mill had indicated through his mental crisis of 1826—is that it is hopelessly *abstract*.

Macpherson presents Mill as pioneering a model of 'developmental democracy', and this model clearly arises as a response to the contradictory character of utilitarian analysis. If, as we have seen, the pursuit of happiness simply amounts to a process of maximising productivity so that some enjoy pleasure while others endure the pain, then there is indeed something highly artificial and unnatural about the felicity calculus. Mill is faced with a situation in which utilitarian capitalism appears to subvert its own principles.

An 'equitable' principle of property requires that the harder people work, the greater should be their rewards. Yet, as Mill points out in his *Principles of Political Economy* (and it is a passage which Marx, 1970, p. 610, cites with approval), the more disagreeable and exhausting their work, the more impoverished workers are likely to be. The 'principle of property' requires that all should be entitled to the property they have produced. Yet, although Mill argues (with some difficulty) that capitalists are entitled to a share of what others produce, he finds their share grossly disproportionate. Moreover this right (to hire the labour power of others) is defensible only if it rests upon free consent and fair exchange. But can freedom and fairness be said to exist in situations in which 'the generality of labourers' have as little choice of occupation or freedom of movement, and are as dependent upon fixed rules and the will of others, as they could be in any system 'short of actual slavery' (Macpherson, 1977, pp. 53–5)?

By continuing to skate over the radical differences which divide workers from capitalists, Benthamite utilitarians failed to see that propertyless people cannot be said to pursue meaningful or pleasurable interests since (strictly speaking) they have yet to *acquire* them. Their 'individuality' is so abstract that it is still to be awakened! Hence Mill insists in *On Liberty* that utility must now be understood 'in the largest sense' as an ethic grounded in the permanent interests of people as 'progressive beings'. Human nature, as he puts it in a celebrated passage, is not a machine to be built after a model, but a tree which requires to grow and develop itself on all sides (1974, p. 70; p. 123). Happiness, in other words, is not static but *developmental*. As long as 'some are born to riches and the vast majority to poverty' (Mill, 1964, p. 167), happiness is not something which most people will be in a position to pursue. In stressing that humans are exerters and developers (and not simply consumers and appropriators), Mill makes it possible, Macpherson argues, to move from a 'protective' to a 'developmental' model of liberal democracy.

Yet the transition from Model One to Model Two is still fraught with irony and contradiction. It is precisely because Mill is so conscious of deepening class divisions (in a way which Bentham and his father were not), that he fears the social consequences of the working class vote. Atomised workers may well accept the abstract egalitarianism—the metaphysical subtleties and theological niceties—of the exchange process, but organised workers will not. Their struggles bring them of necessity face to face with the radical inequalities of power which underpin these alluring abstractions. Chartism had already declared the vote 'a knife and fork question', and in a Britain which had experienced the bitterness and conflict of the Hungry Forties, Mill finds himself less and less able to support democracy. He has come to dread (as he tells us in the rather painful prose of the Victorian middle classes) 'the ignorance and especially the selfishness and brutality of the mass' (1964, p. 167).

In his *Considerations of Representative Government*, he advocates the exclusion of paupers, bankrupts, illiterates and non-taxpayers from the franchise, and argues the case for a system of plural voting which would mean that employers and professional people had more votes than those lower down the class hierarchy (Macpherson, 1977, p. 58). If the 'brutalised mass' will not spontaneously follow the lead of the virtuous middle rank, then the distribution of votes must be skewed to take this into account.

It would appear then Mill has simply retreated from the position of the utilitarians. Confronted by a radical conflict of interest among supposedly 'abstract individuals', he abandons even the universal male suffrage posited in the protective model. Yet it might be argued that in some ways this retreat is deceptive, for at least Mill has addressed himself directly to the problem of power and inequality in a class divided society. Perhaps this is why Held contends rather curiously that, unlike Bentham and his father, Mill was 'a clear advocate of democracy' (1987, p. 86). He has been compelled to develop a more dynamic view of human nature which highlights the fact that a democracy is really possible only when the problem of power and inequality has itself been resolved.

Hence the contradictory formulation of the *Autobiography*. While less of a democrat than he had been, he tells his readers, 'our ideal of ultimate improvement went far beyond democracy, and would class us [i.e. Mill and his wife Harriet Taylor] decidedly under the general designation of socialists' (1964, p. 167). Despite his fear of popular rule, Mill could still support the case for producer cooperatives and women's rights. This is why Macpherson argues that although Mill's model is a step back from Model One in arithmetic terms, 'in its moral dimension' it is actually more democratic (1977, p. 60). But here we must tread with caution.

In the first place, as we have seen, the utilitarian model (leaving aside the exclusion of women from the suffrage) is itself only apparently democratic. It concedes majority rights as a way of entrenching minority power. It is true that its abstract premises are internally subversive (in the time-honoured liberal fashion), and we have seen how Mill, in reacting against the 'schizoid malady' of abstract utilitarianism, is compelled to adopt a more dynamic and developmental view of individuality.

But if Mill is more concrete in his approach, is he not less *democratic*? Not only does he explicitly erect elitist barriers against what he sees as the dangers of 'class legislation' (i.e. laws which would specifically advance working class interests). As part of his reaction against abstract individualism, he accepts that in the case of the colonies, 'despotism' is a 'legitimate mode of government in dealing with barbarians' (1974, p. 69). In the name of self-development, a veto is given, as Macpherson puts it (1977, p. 60), to those who are more developed—both within Britain and abroad.

It seems odd to say therefore, as Macpherson does, that a model which in some ways entrenches the power of property even more explicitly than before, is (at least in moral terms) a further step towards democracy. Mill may have been sympathetic to what he calls 'socialistic experiments by select individuals' (1964, p. 169) but then so too were the Tory critics of the industrial revolution. Indeed so impressed was the young Friedrich Engels by Thomas Carlyle's romantic onslaught on liberal capitalism in *Past and Present* that he regarded this reactionary Tory as the virtual devotee of a 'philosophical communism' (Hoffman, 1983, p. 28). Individuality does not wholly cease to be abstract just because it becomes developmental. For we need to continually press the question: just *who* precisely are the individuals to be developed?

It is true that Mill was moving away from a negative and towards a positive liberalism, and that he had pioneered a number of important conceptual advances along the way. A more dynamic view of human nature, a more concrete view of individuality, and, as we noted in our previous section, a broad social view of the question of coercion. These conceptual developments flow logically from (while moving beyond) the subversive abstractions of the liberal tradition, and they impress themselves upon people's minds as the socially divisive character of capitalism itself becomes increasingly evident.

But it cannot be said, as Macpherson seems to suggest, that in themselves these advances are democratic. Mill's position shows quite dramatically that a move towards positive liberalism may actually be a move *away* from democracy: it may represent an orientation towards an elitism far more explicit than liberals had ever accepted before. Positive liberalism may be less abstract than negative liberalism but why should this in itself make it more democratic? Positive liberals have certainly become conscious of the concrete social power which underpins the formal equalities of abstract rights, but this insight may (at least under some circumstances) merely reinforce support for elite rule.

The fact then that Mill endorsed a developmental view of individuality does not (by itself) signal the transition from liberalism to democracy. Hence we must conclude by insisting that the tension between our two conceptual partners still stands. The question of whether a 'liberal democracy' is actually possible—and not merely a contradiction in terms—remains to be tackled in our final chapter.

9 Democracy—'A Name For What We Cannot Have'?

LIBERAL REFORMISM AND THE ADVANCE TO DEMOCRACY

We have argued so far that what exacerbates the difficulty of getting to grips with the concept of democracy is its relationship with liberalism. By abstracting individuals from social and political hierarchies, liberalism mystifies the state but in a highly subversive way. If people can govern themselves in a state of nature, why should they tolerate repressive and inegalitarian institutions in society? Liberalism itself appears to imply the need for democracy. Yet because its subversive premises are also abstract, they conceal (as we have already indicated) very real hierarchies of power. Once liberals begin to analyse politics more concretely, class divisions and elite rule become obvious for all to see.

How then are liberals to respond to the 'schizoid malady' which threatens? They might of course become reactionaries and explicitly reject democracy. But this poses serious problems for the liberal identity, for in thoroughly exorcising the subversive potential of their own theory, reactionary liberals become virtually indistinguishable from authoritarian conservatives.

Another line of argument is possible. Why not tackle this problem by moving *towards* democracy rather than away from it? Why can't liberals utilise the kind of conceptual advances we noted with Mill so that freedom and equality leave their theological heaven and come down to earth? Why not, in other words, resolve the tension between abstract promise and concrete reality in a radical rather than conservative way? Thus Macpherson argues (1977, p. 2) that if we de-emphasise the traditional market assumptions of liberalism, something which can be properly called a 'liberal democracy' appears on the horizon. But is this really so? Can liberals become democrats without transcending their liberalism altogether?

To explore this problem further we must follow Macpherson as he moves to a variant of Mill's model in which Mill's followers cheerfully abandoned the inegalitarian provisions of his (seemingly eccentric) elitism. Eleven years after Mill's death the suffrage was substantially broadened. By the end of the First World War Britain had universal male suffrage and ten years later, votes for all women as well. Mill's elitist qualifications were not only unacceptable to popular movements, they also appeared unnecessary. Class rule by propertyless workers did not materialise as Mill had feared (and Marx and Engels had once hoped). On the contrary, the democratic franchise was 'tamed', and Macpherson gives two reasons for this development.

The first he ascribes to the rise of the modern party system. This he says, has had the effect of shielding 'existing property institutions and the market system' from attack (1977, p. 66). Each party finds that in order to win elections it has to project itself as a national organisation representing the common good, and this has meant in practice diluting class politics in favour of a moderating middle ground. A mass electorate encourages the growth of centrally controlled party machines so that the necessary compromising, manoeuvring and the blurring of issues can be carried through with relatively little popular participation from below.

Macpherson concedes, however, that something as 'mechanical' as a system of competing parties could not in itself have succeeded in neutralising the potentially radical impact of the propertyless vote. The blurring and the moderating, the compromising and the manoeuvring had to produce some tangible benefit for the subordinate classes, and indeed it did—it produced reform. As early as 1847, the Ten Hours Bill in Britain was passed in the teeth of fierce opposition from the 'old' liberals, and Marx hailed the Act as a victory 'for the political economy of the working class' (Hoffman, 1984, p. 134).

The New Liberals (like T.H. Green and L.T. Hobhouse) accepted the need for trade unions; sanitary and health acts; land and tax reform; unemployment and accident insurance; and policies which generally sought a more equitable distribution of wealth in society. Theorists like Lindsay and McIver, Dewey and Barker were now critical of the old abstract individualism, and they supported the case for a welfare state. Dewey spoke of the need to introduce 'social responsibility into our business system', and even argued that liberalism should 'socialize the forces of production' (Macpherson, 1977, p. 74). There can be no denying New Liberal enthusiasm and commitment for social reform. Hobhouse spoke for all the New Liberals when he declared in 1911 that without change, liberalism would become 'fossilised as an extinct form' (1964, p. 110).

The New Liberals were still, of course, new *liberals*. Even when they followed Mill and Hobhouse in espousing a creed of 'liberal socialism', they saw themselves as fighting for freedom against 'class interests'. Reformists they certainly were, but were they democrats? Unlike Mill, they *seemed* to have little hesitation in endorsing democracy. They supported universal suffrage, and described democracy as 'the necessary basis of the Liberal idea' (Hobhouse, 1964, p. 116)—a humanist ethic infusing every phase of 'our culture' (Macpherson, 1977, p. 75). Yet we return to our basic problem. How was this democratic ethic to be realised in a class-divided society? How far could the reform process proceed before coming up against the conflict between capital and labour, and all its attendant social and political hierarchies?

Here it has to be said that the relationship between the New Liberals and Mill is as problematic as Mill's relationship to his own utilitarian forebears. In one sense Mill, as we have seen, went beyond Benthamism by recognising the intractable character of class divisions, and yet of course, this is precisely the reason why he reteated from democracy. The New Liberals on the other hand appeared to go beyond Mill in supporting democracy, but they did so precisely because they believed that the process of reform was dissolving away the divisions of class. If Mill retreated from democracy, they retreated from realism.

A.L. Lindsay says of Green and his fellow liberals that they were political democrats because they were 'first of all spiritual democrats'. As far as (most) New Liberals were concerned, democracy must be based on religion (Green, 1941, p. x). They saw society in terms of a community of interest—a 'general will' which transcended class conflict—and Hobhouse specifically attacked revolutionary socialists for their belief in class war. Modern society, he argued, exhibits a 'complex interweaving of interests' so that clear-cut distinctions between the classes do not exist (1964, p. 88). This is why, as Macpherson notes, the New Liberals found the cut-and-thrust, give-and-take of the modern party system congenial. In their eyes, it appeared to broaden the spread of freedom and equality, and obliterate distinctions of class (1977, p. 70).

All this would seem to suggest that the old metaphysical subtleties and theological niceties of the classical tradition had been brushed aside only to reappear in a new form. Indeed nowhere is the abstract and otherwordly character of the New Liberalism more apparent than in its enthusiastic endorsement for the mediating and moderating role of the *state*.

As far as the New Liberals are concerned, the state stands as a social bulwark against selfish private interests. It is the state or (at least as Green put it) the 'true state' which has the primary function of enacting laws equally in the interests of all (1941, p. 129). The commitment to a 'spiritual democracy' expresses itself in that most theological of concepts—'the self-governing State' (Hobhouse, 1964, p. 25; p. 81). The state which punishes, imprisons and divides in the name of the community as a whole rests nevertheless upon 'will' rather than 'force'. The roots of this political mystification lie (as we have seen) in the abstractions of the exchange process. It comes therefore as no surprise to learn that behind the grand abstraction of the 'self-governing individual in the self-governing state', there lurks the independent owner of private property.

For Green, the mainstay of social order and contentment is 'a class of small proprietors tilling their own land' (1906, p. 378). Hobhouse considers that a class of independent peasants must be reconstituted as 'the backbone of the working population'. They should be tenants rather than landlords; a

'State tenantry' who are rewarded with the fruits of their own work—and no more (1964, p. 92). But what of the capital-labour relationship, the relationship which combines legal equality with social despotism?

The New Liberals followed Mill in rejecting the idea that private capital is inherently exploitative. Workers, they accept, would still have to sell their labour power to make a living, but they insisted that they should do so in conditions of security and independence so that contracts could be based upon a real equality between partners. Capitalism (it might be said) was not to be abolished so much as it was to be diffused among the community as a whole (Arblaster, 1984, p. 288). With the help of the state and welfare regulation, the liberal ideal of the 'self-made man' could at last become a reality.

Accompanying an uncritical view of the capital-labour relationship, was the belief in 'liberal' patriarchy. Of course women should vote as citizens, and enjoy all the rights of the fully responsible individual. But Green could still take it for granted that the man is the head of the family (1906, p. 375), while Hobhouse argues that women should be encouraged (through public remuneration) to stay at home and mind the children (1964, p. 94). The marital contract is to become 'fairer' while the structural inequalities of power remain.

Underpinning this New Liberal reformism is yet another hierarchy. This hierarchy is less explicit perhaps than the others, but it is one which has to be grasped if sense is to be made of the ameliorating project as a whole. For what makes it possible to blunt class antagonisms through reforms? A positive role for the state costs money, and as we have seen, the notion of a common interest and general will forged through party competition seems plausible only if it yields greater material and social security to those without property. Indeed it is worth recalling that in the late ninteenth century it was not only liberals who had become converts to the democratic franchise. So had conservatives. 'Tory democrats' like Disraeli made it clear that 'elevating the condition of the people' rests upon capitalist expansion and 'upholding' the Empire (Gilmour, 1978, p. 83). As Macpherson rightly emphasises, had it not been for continental expansion in North America and imperial expansion by Britain and most of Western

Europe, the apparently neutral party system could not have tamed the franchise (1977, p. 67). It is hardly a coincidence then that those who favoured reform were becoming at the same time (as Hobhouse puts it), 'Imperialists in their sleep' (1964, p. 113). Liberals may have been advancing towards democracy, but at whose expense?

We have already noted Mill's support for 'enlightened' despotism in the colonies. On this point Hobhouse is also revealing. For while he warns of the dangers which imperialism abroad poses for liberties at home—'a democrat cannot be a democrat for his own country alone'—he nevertheless equivocates. He cannot make up his mind, for example, whether to support home rule for the Irish (1964, p. 26; p. 113). He invokes the old liberal prejudice against servants and dependents to bolster an argument that as far as the Crown colonies are concerned, it may be that a 'semi-despotic system' is the best that can be devised (1964, p. 120; p. 26). The New Liberal democracy, it would seem, is 'spiritual' in character because when it comes down to earth it obviously cannot embrace everybody.

Even among the apparent champions of the democratic ideal, doubts and reservations surface. Hobhouse fears that the doctrine of popular sovereignty might lead to the 'expropriation of the rich', and he wonders whether 'from the general point of view of liberty and social progress', a limited franchise might not yield better results than one that is extended (1964, p. 28). True, a 'spiritual democracy' postulates the existence of a unifying social interest. But the 'inherent difficulty' of democratic government is that it is government by majority, not government by 'universal consent'. Both the suspensory veto of a Second Chamber and the right of the House of Commons to submit matters to referendum would constitute salutary checks upon 'a large and headstrong majority' (1964, p. 124). Hence, as Freeden (1978, p. 126) notes, the New Liberals saw themselves as justifying reform through a common social interest rather than in terms of 'the democratic argument'.

In other words, the traditional liberal fear of popular rule still lingers. It is only a few, Hobhouse tells us, who can be expected to be fully absorbed in public affairs. As far as the democrat is concerned, it is this remnant which 'saves the people' (1964, p. 117). The elitism of Hobhouse may be more genteel and diplomatic than the elitism of Mill but it still serves to underscore our general point. The term 'liberal' qualifies democracy (Ruggiero, 1959, p. 379)—and necessarily so. For after all, liberalism is about the rights of property, while democracy is about popular rule.

Indeed, Ruggiero (as an admirer of Hobhouse) acknowledges the class basis of the New Liberalism in fairly matter of fact terms. The strength of the Liberal party, he declares (in a particularly billowy passage), must consist in quality rather than quantity. It must choose its recruits from among those who can understand the value of freedom, human personality and spiritual autonomy; who are independent, respect the law and are self-critical; who can realise the dominion of thought over the inferior activities of the mind. And who are these distinguished beings? Why naturally 'the middle classes' (1959, p. 440)! Mill's 'salt of the earth'; his father's 'virtuous rank'—the source of all that has refined and exalted human nature. Democracy is acceptable only if it does not endanger the power and privileges of this 'civilising' elite. No one can doubt the fervour with which New Liberals championed the need for greater social equality. But is there anything in their argument which (when all is said and done) really challenges the elder Mill's view that the business of government is the business of the rich?

It is true that the 'old' abstraction of the atomistic individual has yielded to the 'new' abstraction of the self-governing state. But we must still press our question. Is this enough to tranform liberals into democrats? While reforms help to humanise the propertied system, beneath the New Liberal abstractions all the old hierarchies—of capital and labour, men and women, coloniser and colonised—still remain.

ELITIST DEMOCRACY: A VICTORY FOR REALISM?

It is not difficult to see why the idealism and otherworldiness of the New Liberals should have left them vulnerable to attack. The model of 'liberal democracy' which emerges during and after the Second World War prides itself on a tough-minded realism—on an iconoclastic irreverence for all the abstractions (whether 'old' or 'new') of the liberal tradition. The 'schizoid malady' of those who profess democracy in theory only to deny it in practice is to be resolved once and for all. Political analysis, insist these new 'revisionist' democrats, must confront things as they really are.

Given the ambiguities which have dogged the democratic concept from the start—ambiguities which liberal abstractions have done so much to exacerbate—this insistence that democratic theory must confront the hierarachical realities of a divided world in a spirit of sober realism appears as a welcome advance. Certainly Macpherson seems enthusiastic. He finds in the 'equilibrium model' of liberal democracy pioneered by Joseph Schumpeter, a 'substantially accurate' description of how the Western liberal system actually works. It is a model which has been built upon by the careful and extensive empirical investigations of a whole galaxy of highly competent scholars (1977, p. 83). Indeed all this sounds so promising and impressive that it begins to appear as if, at long last, the historic conundrums and paradoxes of the concept of democracy are about to be resolved.

Schumpeter's analysis brings us face to face with the problem of democracy as a form of the state with its clear-cut differentiation between rulers and ruled. Popular rights for some, he argues, have always meant oppression and persecution for others. Democracy has nothing to do with ideals. Because there exists a statist division between the rulers and ruled, there are no ultimate values to which all sections of society can relate. There is nothing about democracy which necessarily makes it desirable. It may well be that in some situations—Schumpeter instances the religious settlement under the military dictatorship of Napoleon 1—the wishes of the people are more fully realised when there is no democracy at all (1947, p. 256).

As far as Schumpeter is concerned then, democracy is nothing more than a 'political method'. It is simply an institutional arrangement for reaching political decisions: it is not an end in itself (1947, p. 242). Given the stark hierarchical divisions which democracy as a form of the state implies, it is perfectly possible, Schumpeter argues, for witches to be hunted down and burnt at the stake or for Jews to be persecuted quite *democratically*. The 'demos' might include a given category of people in one set of circumstances only to exclude them in another. Since all governments discriminate against *some* section of the populace (no system for example allows children to vote), it follows that discrimination *per se* is not undemocratic. *We* may not approve of societies which discriminate against women, Jews, blacks or workers, but that is not the point. Given differences in culture and circumstance, every populace must be allowed to define its own identity (1947, p. 245).

Schumpeter's argument is certainly startling in its iconoclasm but is it as realistic as it sounds? The simple truth is, says Schumpeter, that even in a democracy the people do not govern. Nor can they. They are too emotional and irrational, too parochial and too primitive. Whatever control people may have over their own private lives, the typical citizen yields to prejudice, impulse and to what Schumpeter calls 'dark urges' (1947, p. 262) on entering the political realm. It is therefore only through a definitional sleight of hand that we can we speak of popular rule. Those who rule are the politicians. It is the politicians who raise the issues which determine peoples' lives, and it is the politicians who decide them. What then is a democracy? A democracy is a 'political method' by which these politicians are elected by means of a competitive struggle for the vote. The people do not rule: they merely elect those who do. Democracy is a system of elected and competing elites.

The detailed studies of the 1950s produced masses of data which suggested that for most citizens, politics is a 'remote, alien and unrewarding activity' better left to a relatively small number of professional activists (Dahl, 1961, p. 279). Democracy works best when elected leaderships have a free hand: 'where the rational citizen seems to abdicate, nevertheless angels seem to tread' (Macpherson, 1977, p. 92). But what is the status of 'facts' such as these? Clearly apathy and ignorance exist. But is it true to say that these 'facts' are part of an enduring *reality*?

The classical liberals were only too conscious of facts such as these, and this is why they were pessimistic about the prospects of 'self-government'. Factually (to take Rousseau's argument for a moment), the people are everywhere in 'chains'. But he still holds firm to the 'ideal' that they are also 'born free', so that at the very least these chains can be made 'legitimate'. The facts then are not in dispute: what is in dispute is whether these facts are 'natural' realities (which cannot be changed). Classical liberal theory perceived a tension between the two. The 'facts', as Rousseau sees them, are the hierarchical arrangements of a repressive status quo. The world of nature, on the other hand, points to a reality beyond the 'facts', since (as Rousseau says in reply to Aristotle) if people are 'naturally' slaves, it is only because they have been slaves against nature (1968, p. 52).

We have already complained about the abstract character of this theory of natural rights. It assumes, as we have seen, a static, god-given realm of nature outside of social relationships and historical change. Facts are humanly constructed; natural rights are not. Facts should be laid aside because they come and go; natural rights belong to a 'reality' which endures for ever.

This dichotomy is clearly untenable as it stands. As we argued in our earlier section on power, nature itself changes—indeed this is its most enduring attribute. Our natural rights cannot therefore stand outside of the 'facts' (our everyday social experience). Our rights, to use Rousseau's terminology, must arise through the 'facts' since they are historical entitlements which change as humans themselves progress. Yet the classical liberals were still correct to perceive a tension between the two (even if they also mystified it), for there is surely a difference between the 'factual' appearances of everyday life, on the one hand, and the underlying realities of essential social relationships, on the other. These realities (and the 'natural' rights which derive from them) are of course historical in character but they stand as 'natural' (law-governed) historical realities which manifest themselves through the immediately perceptible 'facts' of ordinary experience.

To describe the model of elitist democracy as 'realist' then is to mistake its abstract 'facts' for those wider historical *relationships*—outside of which the 'facts' themselves become illusory and misleading. Indeed, just how abstract some of these 'facts' really are becomes evident if we briefly recall Macpherson's own critique of the equilibrium model.

Post-war liberals liked to present their redefined concept of democracy as an exchange process—a market mechanism with voters as the consumers and politicians as the entrepreneurs. But, as Macpherson himself points out, this ostensible exercise in political realism suggests a kind of perfect competition, an optimum distribution of political energies and political goods which the facts themselves belie. On the supply side, a few sellers (i.e. competing party leaderships) can manipulate demand. On the demand side, competition is equally 'unfair'. The more resources consumers have, the more vigorously they can register their preferences. Hence the higher socio-economic classes participate much more 'cost-effectively' than the lower classes. The inequalities are not therefore (as Dahl has claimed) 'dispersed' in character: they are structural and cumulative.

There exists in others words what Macpherson calls a 'class differential in apathy' (1977, pp. 87–8). Inequality reinforces apathy and apathy reinforces inequality. This can imply only that apathy is not 'natural' but contrived. A more egalitarian distribution of wealth; the provision of better education, health and welfare; an emphasis upon popular participation in decision making at all levels, and we would soon begin to dispel the 'dark urges' and irrational impulses which apparently paralyse the political capacity of the mass of the population.

In terms of Macpherson's own argument then, the equilibrium model is not 'factually accurate' at all. Because we are confronted with a system which produces an equilibrium of a highly unequal kind, this can only, in Macpherson's words, 'put some strain on the claim' (1977, p. 91) that the model is democratic. For all its emphasis on the facts, it actually represents a serious distortion of the power relationships of the real world.

Our 'philosophical' point therefore is this. Although the iconoclasm of the elitists sometimes appears as a refreshing contrast to the sanctimonious moralism of earlier liberals, it has to be said that ultimately the 'equiliberals' were even less realistic than their classical forebears. The latter had at least worked with a concept of human nature which had some insight into essential relationships underlying the 'facts': a concept which had some feel for (although it still mystified) the historically dynamic character of social development. The elitists, on the other hand, appealed to human nature in order to justify cynically a world of frozen hierarchies.

We may put the comparison like this. Whereas the classical liberals (and to some extent the New Liberals as well) constructed their argument on the basis of subversive abstractions, the 'equiliberals' sought to base their argument on abstractions alone; on premises all the *more* remorselessly and mystifyingly abstract because they appeared shorn of the last subversive vestiges of the classical tradition.

Of course there is a dismal continuity which runs through all this degenerative change. Conservative social and political hierarchies, as we have seen, are inherent in the abstractions of the exchange process from the start. Those who are unable to look beyond the contradictory nature of a capitalist society must sooner or later come to terms with these hierarchies. They come 'of age' by discarding with a worldly wise weariness the subversiveness of their youth. The elitists—as it has been said of Max Weber—are 'liberals in despair' (Held, 1987, p. 144), and they reflect the historical exhaustion of a theoretical tradition whose abstract nature begins to overwhelm its once critical dimensions.

We are now in a position to get to grips with that astonishing *volte face* which comes to a head with the democratic theorising of the post-war period. For what were once liberal criticisms of democracy become the prerequisites of democracy itself—a process of conceptual redefinition in which none of the old reservations have disappeared. Schumpter complains that the electorate is incapable of any action other than a stampede, and urges that a ban be placed on the practice of bombarding members of parliament with letters and telegrams (1947, p. 283; p. 295). All this in the name of democracy. Democracy in other words becomes hopelessly ambiguous as liberalism becomes unprecedently abstract.

But why does liberalism increasingly retreat into its world of mystifying abstractions? Just as nineteenth-century Social Darwinists sought to ward off populist challenges by identifying democracy with a capitalism red in tooth and claw, so (as we noted earlier) the development of the cold war with its dogmatic anti-communism played a crucial role in engendering support for the new model of elitist democracy.

The post-war world saw a resurgence of confidence in business leadership. Economies primed on war production could now provide full employment and the rudiments of a welfare state. Further reform seemed unnecessary, and in order to keep the 'threat' of communism at bay, it appeared vital to present the liberal West as the bastion of democratic virtue. A challenge to corporate concentrations of private power, domestically as well as internationally, could be plausibly resisted, however, only if the traditional tension between liberalism and democracy (still evident in some of the positions of the New Liberals) was conceptually obliterated.

It is worth remembering that the cold war 'equiliberals' (unlike their classical counterparts) perceived no particular threat from the political right. For all the ritualistic denunciations of right-wing as well as left-wing 'totalitarianism', it is not difficult to detect in their position a new sympathy and understanding for authoritarian regimes of a conservative kind. After all, Schumpter himself had suggested that in certain circumstances, dictatorships might better serve the popular interest than democracies, and, Dahl, in a work which argues that democracy is a system in which 'minorities rule' follows Schumpter's contention that the politically active themselves decide who is to enjoy legitimacy as participants in the decision-making process. Democracy, it would seem, is possible even when women have no vote, blacks are denied political rights and the communists are shut out in the cold. Indeed even apartheid South Africa is described by Dahl as only 'possibly excepted' from inclusion as a 'polyarchy' (1956, p. 138; p. 74). The odd authoritarian ally of the 'free world' is not the problem. The real threat arises from the 'totalitarianism' or the 'totalitarian democracy' (as it was occasionally called) of the anti-colonialist movements and the socialist states of the post-war world.

This is the context in which the classical heritage is

drastically redefined. The abstractions are retained while every effort is made to ditch their subversive character. Liberalism begins to transform itself into a creed of conservative reaction as it retreats from rationality and affirmative individualism in the name of highly abstract 'facts'. True, the elite democrats engage hierarchical divisions (rather than smother them in a New Liberal humbug of the General Will and the Common Good). But they do so nevertheless in a way which threatens to obliterate the historic tension between liberalism and democracy. This is what makes the equilibrium model so exceptionally mystifying.

FROM ELITISM TO PARTICIPATION: DEMOLISHING THE HIERARCHIES

It has been argued by some that the elite democratic model confronts its critics with a Hobson's choice. Either we are realistic and settle for elitism, or we are idealistic and indulge our preference for democracy (Bachrach, 1967, p. 196). As long as the problem is presented in this way, no conceptual progress is possible. After all, if the real world is as elitist as the 'equiliberals' argue, how can we expect people to participate in government—to run their own lives?

Earlier critiques of democratic elitism reflect this dilemma by simply turning the model inside out. Herbert Marcuse's *One Dimensional Man* (1964) is a case in point. It angrily denounces the equilibrium model as a demonic success depoliticising the public so that they become mere pawns in the grip of the bureaucrats and manipulators. In the same way, Mills's *Power Elite* attacks the concentrations of power in post-war America but can find no social basis for a democratic alternative. This is still the problem (I would argue) with Ralph Miliband's *State in Capitalist Society* (1969): a more conventionally Marxist critique of democratic elitism dedicated to the memory of C. Wright Mills.

Miliband argues (we briefly encountered part of his analysis in Part Two) that in the advanced capitalist regimes of Western society, an economically dominant class exercises a decisive degree of political power. A combination of sympathetic state bureaucrats from within and structural pressures from without is able to neutralise any government mandated by its electors to introduce radical change. As a consequence, socialist politicians are either integrated into the system, or find themselves stranded 'outside' in a ghetto of isolation and despair. To Macpherson's question, 'Can liberal-democratic governments be made more participatory and if so, how?' (1977, p. 94), there appears no answer.

To tackle this problem, we need to raise another. Just how democratic *is* the equilibrium model anyway? Its critics all say 'not very!' but more than just 'quantitative' assessments are needed if the quest for an alternative is to progress. The elitist model may not be 'very' democratic, but it is certainly *liberal*, and we have already noted the way in which it continues to reflect the mystifying abstractions of the exchange process. These liberal qualities constitute (as we noted in our previous section) a rather pale shadow of the subversive subtleties and theological niceties of the classical tradition, but we need to get to grips with them all the same if we are to assess the democratic calibre of the equilibrium model.

The electors, insist the equiliberals, must be allowed a choice—even though both Schumpeter and Dahl equivocate as to whether universal suffrage is necessary before this choice can be exercised democratically. There must be 'free competition for a free vote', says Schumpeter (1947, pp. 271–2). By being able to choose between competing politicians, otherwise passive citizens can at least protect themselves against tyrannical and immovable rulers. But while, as Macpherson points out (1977, p. 91), no one should belittle the importance of this argument for 'protection against tyranny', is this enough to make the model democratic? At what point do *liberal* qualities become democratic ones? This is the nettle which any effective critique of the elitist model compels us to grasp.

Miliband, for example, identifies his advanced capitalist regimes (somewhat reluctantly) as 'bourgeois democratic'. This description, he tells us, is intended to suggest that these are regimes in which an economically dominant class rules *through* democratic institutions rather that 'by way of dictatorship' (1973, p. 21). Advanced capitalist regimes are distinguished by political competition on a more-than-one party basis, the right of opposition, regular elections, representative assemblies, civil guarantees, etc (1973, p. 21). But in what sense can it be said that these (undeniably liberal) regimes are *democratic* in character when, arguably, it is only a propertied minority who actually rule?

Miliband's response to this question is confused—and yet revealing. The civic and political liberties which exist under 'bourgeois democracy' are, he asserts, limited and contingent. Nevertheless, he insists, they constitute an important and valuable element of life in advanced capitalist societies. They materially affect 'the encounter between the state and citizen, and between the dominant classes and the subordinate ones'. Accordingly, it would be extremely dangerous to believe that these 'bourgeois freedoms' are of no consequence at all (1973, pp. 238–9).

But why should 'bourgeois liberties' be valuable and important if they are limited and hypocritical? Why call them 'democratic' when they co-exist with, and can even be used to mystify ideologically (as Miliband emphasises) the concentrated power of business and financial elites? If these freedoms are democratic, how do we account for the fact that they flourish in capitalist oligarchies?

At the heart of Miliband's dilemmas lies our old friend, the subversive liberal abstraction. Yet again we must probe its metaphysical subtleties and theological niceties if we are to find the necessary link between the conservative model of the equiliberals and the participatory model which is to transcend it.

The roots of our problem lie, as we have seen, in the abstractions of the exchange process. It is because the exchange process is abstract that an equality of *rights* masks an inequality of power. If there is a mystifying harmony between power and rights, there is also real tension. An equality of rights inevitably arouses expectations in theory only to dash them in practice. Hence it must of necessity provoke a countervailing response from the victims of this egalitarian hypocrisy.

Marx illustrates this point in his analysis of the worker-capitalist relation. In selling their labour power, workers move out of the atomistic world of individualistic exchanges into the self-evidently social world of production. In order to survive even as the market vendors of labour power, workers have to combine and organise, if only (in the first instance) to ensure 'fair' price for their commodity. To enjoy individual rights, in other words, propertyless workers have to exercise *collective* power, thus invoking what Marx calls 'standards entirely foreign to commodity production' (1970, p. 586). To remain liberals, they must become embryonic socialists. It is here, in this tension between rights and power—a tension which is inherent in exchange process—that the linkage between democracy and liberalism is forged. Capitalism *compels* workers to begin to exercise some power over their own lives in order simply to survive as the vendors of labour power. Hence as a 'self-dissolving contradiction', the system creates the demand for democracy from within the contractual heart of its liberal exchanges.

This is why the legal equality of the employee generates a demand for the political equality of the citizen. It is not just a result of abstract logic; it is the product of a contradictory social reality. The propertyless worker cannot rest content with the vote for its own sake: unless, as the Chartists said, the vote is a knife and fork question, of what use is it to a proletarian whose individuality is not a condition to be protected but a reality still to be attained? The demand for democracy arises from within liberal capitalism as part of the process by which the 'weapons' of the bourgeoisie (their liberal rights) are turned against them. If the reforms which workers win under capitalism represent victories for the 'political economy of the working class', this is because each reform, however insignificant in itself, brings explicitly social criteria to bear upon a system of individualistic exchanges. The old Liberalism yields to the New Liberalism, and the New Liberalism in turn creates the momentum for socialism.

But here we need to be absolutely clear. Liberalism creates democracy in precisely the same way that capitalism creates its own grave-digger. Its abstractions are subversive because they are inherently self-transcending. Of course capitalism as a contradictory social system can sustain a goodly number of victories for the political economy of the working class before it ceases to be capitalism. This is why the critics of the system's reformism are right to be sceptical. Even the equilibrium democrats can find some space within their model for what Karl Popper calls 'piecemeal engineering' rather than 'holistic change'. Seymour Lipset was to argue in 1963 that 'the workers have achieved political citizenship; the conservatives have accepted the welfare state' (Held, 1987, p. 225). A statement like this, however, would lack even its superficial plausibility were it not for the fact that the liberal 'freedom to choose' brings with it democratic consequences. It sharpens and aggravates the contradictory logic of the system—a system that compels workers to organise, politicians to plan, and the 'minimal state' to intervene increasingly in an attempt to stabilise the economy and diffuse social tensions. Even Joseph Schumpeter, it should be remembered, was a reluctant socialist (Held, 1987, p. 169).

But at what point does liberalism become democratic? As long as the subversive logic of democracy remains subordinate, must we not insist with the ancients that oligarchy, and not democracy, still prevails? This is a point upon which Macpherson's model of a participatory democracy throws a good deal of light.

By the 1960s the 'post-war miracle' had begun to wear thin. Apathy, once prized as a source of stability and an expression of consensus, was turning to alienation. Social and racial tension; student protest and peace movements; a new concern for the environment; workers' control and women's liberation—all these developments signalled the fact, as Macpherson notes, that capitalism itself was experiencing economic difficulties of 'near-crisis proportions' (1977, p. 106). The hierarchies complacently justified in the Age of Celebration are now challenged by the new Age of Critique. Elitism and apathy give way to the widespread demand for *participation*. But how is this participation possible in a world in which inequalities induce apathy and apathy perpetuates inequality? Macpherson locates three loopholes within this vicious circle, and these three loopholes illustrate well the 'transcendental' character of the liberal right to choose—that residue of the subversive abstraction which survives in elitist democratic analysis.

Let us begin, Macpherson argues, with people as they are in

the equilibrium model: infinite consumers willing to let others rule on their behalf provided nothing interferes with their (often extremely modest) material comforts in the 'good society'. How does the vicious circle of apathy and inequality erode? To consume infinitely, one needs a certain quality of life in a decent environment. Pollution and other forms of ecological damage bring consumers face to face with a 'public' problem which cannot be resolved simply by private entrepreneurs or competing political elites (1977, p. 102). That is the first loophole.

From a new concern with the physical environment, the infinite consumer moves to consider the social environment—inner urban decay; the ravages of the property developers; the ill-planned housing estates. All a product of elite politics, bureaucratic paternalism, and a lack of real popular participation from below. And from the social environment in general, the equiliberal consumer becomes conscious of the workplace environment in particular, with its mind-numbing division of labour and conveyor-belt boredom, its managerial hierarchies and despotic disciplines. What about some self-government here? This is Macpherson's second loophole.

Underpinning them is a third: the challenge to the consumer posed by the high rate of inflation of the 1970s, coupled with or followed by a depth of unemployment not seen since the 1930s. Each of these loopholes compels apathetic consumers to become politically involved. We encounter the same 'transcendental' logic which we noted in Marx's analysis of the exploited worker. To remain an individualistic liberal, you must become a socially conscious democrat. Involvement in politics and protest emerge not as a distraction from consumer enjoyments, but as the only way to guarantee them.

The new social movements of the 1970s and 1980s are all rooted then in the (residually) subversive abstractions of postwar liberalism. Of course some of their participants are 'old left' campaigners emerging out of the relative isolation of the 1950s. But what gives these movements their distinctive ideological configuration are the New Left attacks on hierarchy and control; the demand for self-affirmation and participation; and a general suspicion of all established political orders, whether of the right or the left. Autonomy and self-determination: this takes us to the heart of the participatory democratic credo! This is the attraction of the movement over the party; of spontaneity over the state; of extending horizontally rather than vertically, so that those left out in the cold—the exploited third world, the ethnic minorities, the women, the gays, and even the slaughtered animals—can now be brought within campaigning focus as issues of equal concern.

It is not difficult to see why the model of a participatory democracy brings us face to face with the problem of politics. A rhetorical demolition of hierarchies is one thing: getting rid of the state (as we noted in the first part of this book) is quite another. Not surprisingly Macpherson is pessimistic about the prospects for success. For tackling the problem of inequality through greater participation can only bring the new social movements into confrontation with concentrations of power—with entrenched hierarchies which require something rather more than a mere conceptual negation to dissolve them away. The power of multi-national corporations; the secret intelligence agencies of government; the trend towards greater authoritarianism (1977, p. 107): at the root of Macpherson's pessimism is the conceptual problem he prefers to ignore, namely the relationship between a participatory democracy and the institution of the state.

A democratic society, Macpherson argues, requires 'democratic political control' over the uses to which capital and the natural resources of society are put. However, here is the rub. Democratic political control implies democracy organised as a *state*, whereas participatory democrats prefer (as we noted in Part One) to define politics in purely social terms.

Macpherson notes the problem, but proceeds to mystify it. His Model Four advocates a pyramidal system of elected councils, but such a system cannot operate in a 'post-revolutionary situation'. Revolutions, he argues, provoke counter-revolutions (or at least the threat of them), and in this situation democratic control has to give way to central authority. This, for Macpherson, is the fateful lesson of October 1917. Yet in what sense can it be said that 'democratic control' is necessarily at odds with 'central authority'? If democracy is a form of the state, then it is a regime in which the people rule through a monopoly of legitimate force, and anyone exercising a monopoly of legitimate force must necessarily command a good deal of concentrated and centralised power.

Indeed, without this power, it is hard to see a participatory order surviving at all. How else, for example, is Miliband's economically dominant class to be displaced—along with all the sympathetic state bureaucrats who have traditionally serviced its interests? Surely it takes some kind of revolutionary democratic *state* to make popular rule a realistic possibility.

Ultimately the problem of democracy (and its relationship to liberalism) can be tackled only if we link it to the other two concepts of our contentious triad. For what makes democracy particularly difficult to analyse is the fact that it embodies and condenses the dilemmas and paradoxes already encountered in our exploration of power and the state. As long as liberalism and democracy are fused together, these other dilemmas and paradoxes simply compound the problem of popular rule. But what happens when liberalism and democracy being to pull apart? Under these circumstances the concepts of power and the state might actually help to clarify (rather than confuse) the question of democracy, so that at last we can see a gleam of light at the end of the tunnel.

The participatory democrats directed their fire against Schumpeterian elitists who, through the construction of sophisticated and highly abstract models, complacently propagated the virtues of the post-war consensus. But from the late 1970s we have begun to witness the rise of a very different kind of liberalism altogether.

LIBERALISM VS. DEMOCRACY: THE CHALLENGE OF THE NEW RIGHT

The post-war consensus has been built, as we have seen, upon a commitment to full employment and the welfare state. As Keynesian remedies began to falter in the 1970s with rising inflation and falling employment, contradictory social and political pressures intensified from both left and right. On the left, there was growing pressure for greater egalitarianism and popular participation. On the right, support for monetarism and a renewed faith in the miracles of the 'free market'.

The rise of a 'New Right' is significant not simply because of its libertarian critique of the state (which we noted earlier), but because for the first time in over a hundred years, the values of liberalism are now being championed in more or less explicit opposition to the values of democracy. Old Liberal fears like those of Macaulay and (in this regard) J.S. Mill are reviving, and theorists like Hayek and Milton Friedman, seen as eccentric and marginal in the 1960s, have become fashionable with politicians and the 'popular' media.

The New Right attack on democracy is often a veiled one (except in some of the extremist pamphleteering on the fringes)—but it is unmistakeable nevertheless. Take the now influential arguments of Sir Frederick Hayek. Although Hayek sounds like Schumpeter when he states that democracy is not an end in itself but a 'method for achieving certain ends' (1960, p. 106), the analytical focus of his argument is quite different. For Hayek writes not as a positivist who claims to eschew all ethical ends, but as an avowed liberal committed above all to 'freedom'. This is why he contends that cultural and spiritual freedom may well flourish under autocratic rule. Chile is a case in point. Liberty has, in Hayek's view, fared better under Pinochet's military dictatorship than it did under the Popular Unity government of Salvador Allende, overthrown in 1973 (Held, 1987, p. 247; Arblaster, 1984 p. 342). If democracy means 'unlimited government' or the 'unrestricted will of the majority', then Hayek for one is not a democrat.

As far as Hayek is concerned, democracy is only acceptable as a system of government constrained by what he calls the 'rule of law'. Here he resurrects the Old Liberal argument that the law must operate according to 'general principles' which do not 'discriminate', so that any attempt to 'interfere' with the capacity of people to pursue their own ends is oppressive. Policies which favour the poor and the needy are automatically ruled out of court: implementing distributive or social justice can only undermine the unfettered choices of the free market.

The Constitution of Liberty—Hayek's most sustained presentation of his Old Liberal position—appeared in 1959 when consensus politics and support for the welfare state were still riding high. His version of liberalism was 'on the defensive' (1960, p. 7), and hence understandably perhaps, he is unwilling to present the contrast between liberalism and democracy too sharply. By the 1970s, however, some Old Liberals have become openly concerned that even the 'limited' democracy which Hayek favoured in 1959 might undermine the social imperatives of the free enterprise system.

A report by the Trilateral Commission published in the United States in 1975 identifies an 'excess of democracy' as the major problem facing the West, for now it seems that even the (rather modest) right of people to choose those who rule them, poses a problem. Voters are inherently prone to what Samuel Brittan has called 'a lack of budgetary restraint'. Competition among the political elites generates excessive electoral expectations which in turn create continual pressures to expand the public purse (Hodgson, 1984, p. 34). Even an elitist Schumpeterian democracy appears to threaten 'freedom'—i.e. the unrestrained pursuit of profit within a corporate capitalist system.

But these New Right attacks on demands for greater egalitarianism and participation bring us face to face with a problem which we must now tackle directly: the relationship between democracy and the state. For the participatory democrats of the New Left have been disconcerted to find their attacks on statism and hierarchy echoed in the populist rhetoric of the New Right. 'Rolling back the frontiers of the state' has proved a potent vote-catching slogan. The welfare state itself now appears as a bureaucratic and paternalistic affront to the sturdy independence of the (somewhat abstractly conceived) self-governing individual.

The New Right challenge is clear. Either democrats get to grips with the problem of the state, or their participatory aspirations will be torpedoed by a rhetorical anti-statism—the practical consequence of which is to concentrate power even more explicitly than before in the hands of an entrepreneurial elite. Despite the populist manner in which they are presented. New Right policies are designed to weaken trade unions, cut welfare benefits, and utilise high unemployment as a way of punishing the poor and the protesters. Taken together they inevitably create the need to increase continuously the powers of the state. In the late twentieth century the subversive (albeit subordinate) logic of democracy has become firmly entrenched within the contradictory cut-and-thrust of the capitalist economy. This democratic logic cannot be crushed by a restrained Lockean minimalism: nothing less that a Hobbesian Leviathan will do the trick!

Hence anti-statist rhetoric co-exists of necessity with an expanding political coercion which not only attacks the (strictly relative) autonomy of local government and the civil service: iron feelers even project into the personal domain of private morality and family upbringing. Elaborate schemes to privatise public corporations require an extensive interference with the market (at taxpayers' expense) if the dream of a 'popular capitalism' is to be made plausible. Hence the New Right's own peculiar version of the old schizoid malady. The individual is to be 'liberated' through statist and private concentrations of power.

The problem facing the participatory democrat then is this. Democracy is a form of the state. Historically this has been so since ancient times, and it will remain so well into the future. On the other hand, democracy also implies self-government, and popular self-government is possible only when society no longer requires a state. Thus democracy itself is, as we have already seen, conceptually ambiguous. It is a form of the state which looks beyond the state. It is a form of concentrated power which yearns for a world of diffuse power as the solution to its problems. Stress one of these contradictory attributes at the expense of the other, and both are imperilled.

If we take democracy simply as a form of the state, we encounter what might be called 'Dunn's dilemma'. 'Democracy is the *name* for what we cannot have—yet cannot cease to want'. How is it possible, Dunn asks, for people to *rule* their own state (1979, p. 27)? Democracy must therefore imply something more. This is why the participatory democrats are suspicious of statist definitions of politics, and stress the importance of democratising society. But 'redefining politics' will not, of course, get rid of the state. On the contrary, as the reactionary policies of the New Right have shown, participatory movements which sharpen the subversive logic of democracy within capitalism soon find themselves confronted, not merely by the power of large corporations, but by the accelerated momentum towards a Hobbesian Leviathan.

The sad truth is (as we noted earlier) that it takes a state to get rid of the state. What makes the experience of 'existing socialism' so unpalatable to the New Left is the fact that democracy can be introduced only through a political concentration of popular power. Democracy remains fragile and subordinate in the oligarchic world of capitalism: its subversive logic becomes secure only when society's resources are socially owned and controlled. But entrenching this subversive logic is possible only when a new order can protect itself from the ravages of the past. Democracy, in other words, can be realised only through the socialist *state*.

But how does this resolve what we have called Dunn's dilemma—the problem of self-government through divisive and hierarchical rule? In the first part of this book, we encountered the concept of the 'transitional state', and this is a notion which can only help at this point of our argument. For the transitional state is a form of the state which is committed, however problematically, to its own political extinction. This commitment takes us to the heart of what I have called the subversive logic of democracy. The transitional state is only possible in a society which has begun to move beyond the mystifying abstractions of the exchange economy, so that conditions are being created which make it possible for people to *begin* to govern their own lives. But here we need to be clear.

Neither the state nor the market can be abolished. Both can only be *transcended*. In other words, there has to be a practical basis to the solution of our theoretical problem. As long as goods are scarce, markets will be needed: as long as people are structurally divided, the state will be there. The role of democracy is to move people through a transitional state (with its politics to end all politics) towards a real self-government. Without a *political* democracy strong enough to tackle the old concentrations of capitalist power, no *social* democracy is possible. Although Levine wrongly (in our opinion) identifies existing socialist states as 'dictatorships of organisational exploiters' (1987, p. 147), he rightly emphasises the role of democracy in ending the state.

In one sense, this is not a new problem. Hobbes himself had seen monopolies and corporations as worms in the 'entrayles' of the body politics (1968, p. 375), and Rousseau had warned of factual obstruction to the General Will. Both understood that without a strong state, the new social order is stillborn. On the other hand, as liberals rather than democrats, they took the abstractions of the exchange process for granted. Hence they saw the state as part of the solution whereas in fact the state is also part of the problem. Those who are democrats rather than liberals, must go further. Political democracy is only necessary as a 'necessarily disappearing necessity'. As a participatory form of political rule, it must create the basis for its own dissolution, so that the subversive promise of the liberal abstraction finally becomes a concrete social reality. Individuals really do begin to govern their own lives.

Without confronting the question of the state and power, the participatory democrat cannot meet the challenge posed by the rhetorical libertarianism of the New Right. For the point about this demagogic anti-statism is that it simply damages the credibilty of democracy without doing anything to dent the powers of the state. If the New Right seek to undermine democracy in favour of liberalism, the New Left must transcend liberalism in favour of democracy. Crises are notoriously unkind to those who remain mesmerised by abstractions. As social tensions deepen, these abstractions disintegrate. Liberalism is coming increasingly into conflict with democracy. The battle lines are now clearly drawn. Either the subversive logic of democracy moves beyond the mystifying abstractions of liberalism, or the abstractions of liberalism will crush the subversive logic of democracy (or at least attempt to)—with no little help from the concentrated powers of the anti-statist state.

This is why to solve our conceptual problem, we cannot rest content with models of a *liberal* democracy. Linking the two terms in this way (as Old Liberals rightly suspect) simply mystifies the problem. Democracy is only possible when it transcends liberalism, just as popular rule is only possible when it transcends property. It is not enough to note (with

Ruggiero, 1959, p. 370) that in the troubled relationship between democracy and liberalism, there is both continuity and antithesis. For there is not just continuity *and* antithesis. There is continuity *through* antithesis. The continuity is only made possible through a relationship of historical rupture. As Hoffman's *First Law of Philosophical Obscurantism* unfailingly reminds us, democracy and liberalism can only be the 'same' because they are at the same time also very different!

Of all the concepts of our contentious triad, democracy is undoubtedly the most difficult. What makes the problem of democracy so awkward to resolve is that it concentrates the wider paradoxes of politics into one simple and seemingly self-evident political concept. All forms of the state, wrote the young Marx, have democracy for their truth. Grasp democracy, and you will have solved the 'riddle of all constitutions' (1975, pp. 29–31). Once you are able to understand how people can rule *themselves*, then all those conceptual connundrums and perplexing paradoxes which have plagued political theory for so long finally fall away.

Bibliography

Arblaster, A. (1984) *The Rise and Decline of Western Liberalism*, Oxford: Basic Blackwell.

Arendt, H. (1970) *On Violence*, London: Allen Lane.

Aristotle (1962) *The Politics*; Harmondsworth: Penguin.

Bachrach, P. (1967) *The Theory of Democratic Elitism*, Boston, Mass.: Little, Brown.

Bachrach, P. and Baratz, M. (1969) 'Decisions and Non-Decisions: An Analytical Framework' in R. Bell *et al.* (ed.), *Political Power*, New York and London: The Free Press and Collier-Macmillan, pp. 100–9.

Ball, T. (1978) 'Two Concepts of Coercion', *Theory and Society*, **5**, 1978, pp. 97–112.

Barker, E. (1959) *The Political Thought of Plato and Aristotle*, New York: Dover.

Barry, B. (1975) 'The Obscurities of Power', *Government and Opposition*, **10**, 1975, pp. 250–4.

Barry, N. (1981) *An Introduction to Modern Political Theory*, London and Basingstoke: Macmillan.

Bentley, A. (1967) *The Process of Government*, Cambridge, Mass.: Belknap, Harvard University Press.

Bigongiari, D. (ed.) (1953) *The Political Ideas of St. Thomas Aquinas*, New York: Hafner.

Bluhm, W. (1984) *Force or Freedom?*, New Haven and London: Yale University Press.

Bryce, J. (1889) *The American Commonwealth*, vol. 2, London: Macmillan.

Burlatsky, F. (1978) *The Modern State and Politics*, Moscow: Progress.

Burnheim, J. (1985) *Is Democracy Possible?*, Cambridge: Polity.

Carter, A. (1979) *Authority and Democracy*, London: Routledge & Kegan Paul.

Childe, G. (1964) *What Happened in History*, Harmondsworth: Penguin.

Cone, P. (1986) 'The Tribe and the State' in J. Hall (ed.), *States and History*, Oxford: Blackwell, pp. 48–77.

Converse, P. (1965) 'Review of D. Easton's *System Analysis of Political Life'*, *American Political Science Review*, **59**, pp. 1061–2.

Cook, S. (1972) 'Coercion and Social Change' in J. Pennock and J. Chapman (eds), *Coercion*, Chicago and New York: Aldine, Atherton, pp. 107–43.

Cox, A., Furlong, P., and Page, E. (1985) *Power in Capitalist Societies*, Brighton: Harvester Press.

Crenson, M. (1970) 'Non-issues in City Politics: The Case of Air Pollution' in M. Surkin and A. Wolfe (eds), *An End to Political Science*, New York: Basic, pp. 144–66.

Crick, B. (1959) *The American Science of Politics*, London: Routledge & Kegan Paul.

Crick, B. (1982) *In Defence of Politics*, 2nd edn, Harmondsworth: Penguin.

Dahl, R. (1954–5) 'The Science of Politics, New and Old', *World Politics*, **7**, pp. 479–89.

Dahl, R. (1956) *A Preface to Democratic Theory*, Chicago and London: University of Chicago Press.

Dahl, R. (1961) *Who Governs?*, New Haven and London: Yale University Press.

Dahl, R. (1969) 'A Critique of the Ruling Elite Model' in R. Bell *et al.* (eds), *Political Power*, New York and London: The Free Press and Collier-Macmillan, pp. 36–41.

Dahl, R. (1976) *Modern Political Analysis*, 3rd edn, New Jersey: Prentice-Hall.

Dahl, R. (1985) *A Preface to Economic Democracy*, Cambridge: Polity.

Dawisha, K. (1986) 'State and Politics in Developed Socialism' in J. Hall (ed.), *States in History*, Oxford: Blackwell, pp. 211–27.

Day, J. (1963) 'Authority', *Political Studies*, **11**, pp. 257–71.

D'Entreves, A. (1967) *The Notion of the State*, Oxford: Clarendon.

De Ste, Croix, G. (1981) *The Class Struggle in the Ancient Greek World*, London: Duckworth.

Domhoff, G. (1978) *Who Really Rules?*, New Jersey: Transaction.

Dunn, J. (1979) *Western Political Theory in the Face of the Future*, London: Cambridge University Press.

Easton, D. (1949) 'Walter Bagehot and Liberal Realism', *American Political Science Review*, **43**, pp. 17–37.

Easton, D. (1950) 'Harold Lasswell: Policy Scientist for a Democratic Society', *Journal of Politics*, **12**, pp. 450–77.

Easton, D. (1953) *The Political System*, New York: Alfred Knopf.

Easton, D. (1965) *A Framework for Political Analysis*, New Jersey: Prentice-Hall.

Easton, D. (1971a) 'The New Revolution in Political Science' in D. Easton, *The Political System*, 2nd edn, New York: Alfred Knopf, pp. 323–48.

Easton, D. (1971b) 'Continuities in Political Analysis: Behavioralism and Post-Behavioralism' in D. Easton, *The Political System*, 2nd edn, New York: Alfred Knopf, pp. 349–77.

Easton, D. (1981) 'The Political System Besieged by the State', *Political Theory*, **9**, pp. 303–25.

Engels, F. (1972) *The Origin of the Family, Private Property and the State*, London: Lawrence and Wishart.

Fine, B. (1984) *Democracy and the Rule of Law*, London: Pluto.

Finley, M. (1973) *Democracy Ancient and Modern*, London: Chatto and Windus.

Forsyth, M. (1987) 'State' in D. Miller *et al.* (eds), *The Blackwell Encyclopedia of Political Thought*, Oxford: Blackwell, pp. 503–6.

Freeden, M. (1978) *The New Liberalism*, Oxford: Clarendon.

Gallie, W. (1955) 'Essentially Contested Concepts', *Proceedings of the Aristotelian Society*, **56**, pp. 167–98.

Gettell, R. (1928) *History of American Political Thought*, New York: The Century Co.

Gilmour, I. (1978) *Inside Right*, London, Melbourne and New York: Quartet.

Goldman, E. (1955) *Rendezvous with Destiny*, New York: Vantage.

Gramsci, A. (1971) *Selections from the Prison Notebooks*, London: Lawrence and Wishart.

Gray, J. (1983) 'Political Power, Social Theory and Essential Contestability' in D. Miller and L. Siedentop (eds), *The Nature of Political Theory*, Oxford: Clarendon, pp. 75–101.

Green, T. (1906) 'Liberal Legislation and Freedom of Contract' in *Works of Thomas Hill Green*, vol. 3, London, New York and Bombay: Longmans, Green & Co, pp. 365–86.

Green, T. (1941) *Lectures on the Principles of Political Obligation*, London, New York and Toronto: Longmans, Green & Co.

Hall, D. and Madood, T. (1979) 'Practical Politics and Philosophical Inquiry: A Note', *Philosophical Quarterly*, **29**, pp. 340–4.

Hall, S. (1984a) 'The State in Question' in G. McLennan, D. Held and S. Hall (eds), *The Idea of the Modern State*, Milton Keynes and Philadelphia: Open University Press, pp. 1–28.

Hall, S. (1984b) 'The State—Socialism's Old Caretaker', *Marxism Today*, November, pp. 24–9.

Hamilton, A. *et al.* (1961) *The Federalist Papers*, New York: Basic.

Hartz, L. (1955) *The Liberal Tradition in America*, New York: Harcourt, Brace & World Inc.

Hayek, F. (1960) *The Constitution of Liberty*, London and Henley: Routledge & Kegan Paul.

Hegel, G. (1956) *The Philosophy of History*, New York: Dover.

Hegel, G. (1967) *The Philosophy of Right*, Oxford: Clarendon.

Held, D. (1987) *Models of Democracy*, Cambridge: Polity.

Hill, C. (1969) *The Century of Revolution*, London: Sphere.

Hobbes, T. (1968) *Leviathan*, Harmondsworth: Penguin.

Hobhouse, L. (1964) *Liberalism*, London, Oxford and New York: Oxford University Press.

Hodgson, G. (1984) *The Democratic Economy*, Harmondsworth: Penguin.

Hoffman, J. (1983) *Marxism, Revolution and Democracy*, Amsterdam: B.R. Gruner.

Hoffman, J. (1984) *The Gramscian Challenge*, Oxford: Blackwell.

Hofstadter, R. (1967) *The American Political Tradition*, London: Jonathan Cape.

Horton, J. (1984) 'Political Philosophy and Politics' in A. Leftwich (ed.), *What is Politics?*, Oxford: Blackwell, pp. 106–23.

Hughes, C. (1966) 'Professor Leibholz and the Science of Politics' in K. Bracher *et al.* (eds), *Moderne Demokratie und ihr Recht*, Tubingen: J.C. Mohr, pp. 179–89.

Jordan, B. (1985) *The State*, Oxford: Blackwell.

Laver, M. (1983) *Invitation to Politics*, Oxford: Blackwell.

Leftwich, A. (1983) *Redefining Politics*, London and New York: Methuen.

Leftwich, A. (1984) 'Introduction on the Politics of Politics' in A. Leftwich (ed.) *What is Politics?*, Oxford: Blackwell, pp. 1–18.

Levine, A. (1987) *The End of the State*, London: Verso.

Lively, J. (1976) 'The Limits of Exchange Theory' in B. Barry (ed.), *Power and Political Theory*, London and New York: John Wiley, pp. 1–13.

Lively, J. and Rees, J. (1978) *Utilitarian Logic and Politics*, Oxford: Clarendon.

Locke, J. (1924) *Two Treatises of Civil Government*, London: Dent.

Lukes, S. (1974) *Power: A Radical View*, London: Macmillan.

McCloskey, R. (1967) 'Capitalism, Sumnerism and Democracy' in J. Roche (ed.), *American Political Thought*, New York, Evanston and London: Harper & Row, pp. 164–95.

Macpherson, C.B. (1962) *The Political Theory of Possessive Individualism*, London, Oxford and New York: Oxford University Press.

Macpherson, C.B. (1966) *The Real World of Democracy*, New York and Oxford: Oxford University Press.

Macpherson, C.B. (1973) *Democratic Theory*, Oxford: Clarendon.

Macpherson, C.B. (1977) *The Life and Times of Liberal Democracy*, Oxford, London and New York: Oxford University Press.

Macpherson, C.B. (1978) 'The Economic Penetration of Political Theory', *Journal of the History of Ideas*, **39**, pp. 101–18.

Mair, L. (1962) *Primitive Government*, Harmondsworth: Penguin.

Mann, M. (1980) 'The Pre-Industrial State', *Political Studies*, **28**, pp. 297–304.

Mann, M. (1986) 'The Autonomous Power of the State' in J. Hall (ed.), *States in History*, Oxford: Blackwell, pp. 109–36.

Marx, K. (1970) *Capital*, vol. 1, London: Lawrence and Wishart.

Marx K. and Engels, F. (1975) *Collected Works*, vol. 3, London: Lawrence and Wishart.

Marx, K. and Engels, F. (1976a) *Collected Works*, vol. 5, London: Lawrence and Wishart.

Marx, K. and Engels, F. (1976b) *Collected Works*, vol. 6, London: Lawrence and Wishart.

Miliband, R. (1970) 'The Capitalist State: Reply to Nicos Poulantzas', *New Left Review*, **59**, pp. 53–60.

Miliband, R. (1973) *The State in Capitalist Society*, London, Melbourne and New York: Quartet.

Mill, J.S. (1964) *Autobiography*, New York: Signet Classics.

Mill, J. S. (1974) *On Liberty*, Harmondsworth: Penguin.

Mill, J. S. (1976) 'M. de Tocqueville on Democracy in America' in G. Williams (ed.), *John Stuart Mill on Politics and Society*, Glasgow: Fontana, pp. 186–247.

Miller, D. (1983) 'Linguistic Philosophy and Political Theory' in D. Miller and L. Siedentop (eds), *The Nature of Political Theory*, Oxford: Clarendon, pp. 35–51.

Morgan, L. (1964) *Ancient Society*, Cambridge, Mass.: Harvard University.

Mosca, G. (1939) *The Ruling Class*, New York, London and Toronto: McGraw Hill.

Nozick, R. (1974) *Anarchy, State and Utopia*, Oxford: Blackwell.

Oppenheim, F. (1981) *Political Concepts*, Oxford: Blackwell.

Parekh, B. (1968) 'The Nature of Political Philosophy' in P. King and B. Parekh (eds), *Politics and Experience*, Cambridge: Cambridge University Press, pp. 153–207.

Parsons, T. (1969) 'On the Concept of Political Power' in R. Bell *et al.* (eds), *Political Power*, New York and London: The Free Press and Collier-Macmillan, pp. 251–84.

Partridge, P. (1967) 'Politics, Philosophy and Ideology' in A. Quinton (ed.), *Political Philosophy*, Oxford: Oxford University

Press, pp. 32–52.

Plato, (1955) *The Republic*, Harmondsworth: Penguin.

Poulantzas, N. (1973a) *Political Power and Social Classes*, London: New Left Books.

Poulantzas, N. (1973b) 'The Problem of the Capitalist State' in J. Urry and J. Wakeford (eds), *Power in Britain*, London: Heinemann, pp. 291–305.

Pym, F. (1984) 'Testimony of a Wet', *Sunday Times*, June 17, p. 33.

Raphael, D.D. (1976) *Problems of Political Philosophy*, rev. edn, London and Basingstoke: Macmillan.

Ritchie, D. (1895) *Natural Rights*, New York and London: Macmillan and Swan Sonnenschein.

Roberts, S. (1979) *Order and Dispute*, Harmondworth: Penguin.

Rosenberg, A. (1939) *Democracy and Socialism*, Boston: Beacon.

Rothbard, M. (1978a) *For a New Liberty*, rev. edn, New York and London: Collier-Macmillan.

Rothbard, M. (1978b) 'Society without a State' in J. Pennock and J. Chapman (eds), *Anarchism*, New York: New York University Press, pp. 194–207.

Rousseau, J. (1953) *The Confessions*, Harmondsworth: Penguin.

Rousseau, J. (1968) *The Social Contract*, Harmondsworth: Penguin.

Rousseau, J. (1973) *The Social Contract and Discourses*, rev. edn. London: Dent.

Ruggiero, G. de (1959) *The History of European Liberalism*, Boston: Beacon.

Sartori, G. (1973) 'What is Politics?', *Political Theory*, **1**, pp. 5–26.

Schumpeter, J. (1947) *Capitalism, Socialism and Democracy*, 2nd ed, New York and London: Harper.

Shaw, B. (1930) *The Apple Cart*, London: Constable.

Skillen, A. (1977) *Ruling Illusions*, Hassocks: Harvester Press.

Southall, A. (1968) 'Stateless Societies' in *International Encyclopedia of the Social Sciences*, vol. 15, London and New York: Macmillan and The Free Press, pp. 157–67.

Stone, C. (1978) 'Some Reflections on Arbitrating Our Way to Anarchy' in J. Pennock and J. Chapman, *Anarchism*, New York: New York University Press, pp. 208–14.

Strauss, L. (1945) 'On Classical Political Philosophy', *Social Research*, **12**, pp. 98–117.

Taylor, M. (1982) *Community, Anarchy and Liberty*, Cambridge: Cambridge University Press.

Thomson, G. (1955) *Studies in Ancient Greek Society*, vol. 2, London: Lawrence and Wishart.

Tocqueville, A. de (1966) *Democracy in America*, London and Glasgow: Fontana.

Weber, M. (1964) *The Theory of Social and Economic Organisation*, New York and London: The Free Press and Collier Macmillan.

Weldon, T.D. (1953) *The Vocabulary of Politics*, Harmondsworth: Penguin.

Weldon, T.D. (1956) 'Political Principles' in P. Laslett (ed.), *Philosophy, Politics and Society*, 1st series, Oxford: Blackwell, pp. 22–34.

Wood, N. (1978) 'The Social History of Political Theory', *Political Theory*, **6**, pp. 345–67.

Index